The
SERIOUSLY GOOD
KIDS' COOKBOOK

Sue Quinn

quadrille

INTRODUCTION

There's always something cooking in our kitchen. When mum's not testing recipes for cookbooks or making up weird (oops, we mean yummy!) things for dinner, we love to get in there and cook too. That's why we thought it would be fun to do a cookbook together.

Mum wrote all the recipes based on things we like to cook and eat at our house. And we asked all our mates to suggest things they like to cook and eat as well. Then we spent zillions of hours cooking and smiling for the camera while mum took all the photographs.

This book is for kids to cook from. That's why it's called *The Seriously Good* **Kids'** *Cookbook*. You don't have to be a whizz-kid cook – we're just ordinary kids so if we can cook these recipes, so can you! Some of them are harder than others, but if you're aged 8 or older you can have a go at cooking them all by yourself. Just make sure there's an adult nearby to lend a hand if you need it.

Don't worry if things go wrong. (Mum won't let us say how many things we burned while making this book!) Professional cooks make lots of mistakes. In fact, sometimes you can accidentally end up with something delish even when things don't go quite as planned.

We had loads of fun making this book. We hope you have just as much fun making the recipes.

Happy cooking!

Love

Ruby (11) and Ben (8)

Things to eat when you're on the move

When you fancy a challenge

Adults really love this stuff!

THE BITS YOU MUST READ FIRST

HANDY TIPS

 Cooking is a great way to impress your adults. The recipes are designed for kids to cook themselves, but make sure an adult's nearby to help if you get stuck. But, most importantly – HAVE FUN!

EPIC FAIL ALERT!

Always pay close attention to this warning – it contains important tips to prevent things going horribly wrong.

ADULT HELP ALERT!

When you see this warning, **ALWAYS** ask an adult to help you with this step.

HOW TO AVOID EPIC FAILS

* Before you start, read the recipe and make sure you have all the equipment. Also, measure out all of the ingredients first.

* Ask an adult to show you how to use the hob and oven before you start. Burnt or raw food is a major disappointment.

* Each recipe has a difficulty rating in the top left corner: 1 star means it is really simple, 3 stars means that it is slightly trickier.

HOW TO AVOID A KITCHEN DISASTER ZONE

* If you spill something on the floor wipe it up straight away with paper towel – not the cloth you use to wipe the work surface!

* Don't ever cook in bare feet, sandals or flip-flops. If you drop a knife you could be seriously injured.

* **ALWAYS** use oven gloves when handling something hot. We sometimes forgot when putting things in the oven as the dish is not hot, but the oven is, so **NEVER** be as silly or forgetful as we were!

* Put things away as you go.

* Keep a bowl on your work top to chuck rubbish in (like peelings and empty packets). This keeps your surface clear and easy to clean. Empty the bowl into the bin when you've finished.

COOKING TERMS

* **A pinch** – this is a very small amount of something dry or powdered, like salt. Pinch a bit of the ingredient between your thumb and pointing finger.

* **Beat** – to mix something using lots of energy, using a wooden spoon or electric beaters.

* **Boil** – to heat a liquid until big bubbles rise to the top quickly.

* **Butter** – we mean unsalted butter. This way you can decide how much salt to add, if any.

* **Eggs** – we use large eggs, but don't worry, you can use medium.

* **Finely chop** – cut into very small pieces.

* **Measuring cups, teaspoons and tablespoons** – not cutlery or drinking cups, but special cups and spoons used to measure. Scoop up the ingredient and then use a knife to slide across the top to make it level. A "scant" cup means a little bit less than a full cup, and a "generous" cup is a little bit more.

* **Optional** – this might be on the end of an ingredient. It means you can choose to add this to the recipe or not, it is up to you.

* **Set aside** – to leave an ingredient alone while you prepare something else. You'll come back to it later.

* **Set the pan over the heat** – turn the hob to the temperature you need and put the pan on.

* **Simmer** – to heat something almost to boiling point so that very small bubbles (like fizzy drink bubbles) rise to the top slowly.

* **Whisk** – a way of beating quickly and lightly, using a whisk or electric beaters, to fill the ingredient with air.

VERY USEFUL

EQUIPMENT

66 This is all the basic kitchen kit you need to cook the recipes in this book. It's really important to read the recipe first and get out the equipment before you start. 99

CHOPPING BOARDS

VEGETABLE PEELER

COLANDER

WHISK

LEMON SQUEEZER

TIMER

MEASURING SPOONS AND CUPS

MIXING BOWL

PESTLE AND MORTAR

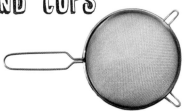

SIEVE

FRYING PAN

FISH SLICE

BAKING TRAY

WOODEN SPOON

PARING KNIFE

SPATULA

OVEN GLOVE

BRUSH

GARLIC PRESS

GRIDDLE PAN

MEASURING JUG

CAKE TIN

LADLE

DISH TOWELS

ROLLING PIN

WEIGHING SCALES

GRATER

SAUCEPAN

TONGS

BAKING SHEET

APRON

HOW TO NOT CHOP OFF YOUR FINGER AND OTHER COOL TIPS

 **A sharp knife is safer than a blunt one as it slices more easily. A blunt knife needs more pressure, so is likely to slip. The techniques shown below can be applied to any ingredient that needs chopping.**

 HOW TO SAFELY HOLD A KNIFE

A sharp paring knife is perfect for kid-size hands. Hold it with your palm down, thumb on one side and pointing finger curved around. **TOP TIP** Don't rest your pointing finger on top of the knife – it might slip off!

HOW TO CHOP AN ONION

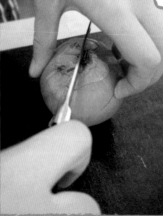

 3 Peel off the papery skin.

4 With your hand in the bridge position, make many vertical cuts in both halves. Don't cut through the root, the slices should stay attached.

1 Place the onion on a chopping board and hold firmly with one hand. Spread your fingers out and tuck them under a bit. This is called the claw position. Slice off the pointy end (not the root end).

2 Place cut-side down. Make a bridge with your hand by placing your thumb on one side of the onion and your fingers on the other. Cut in half.

5 Cut away the root for slices or, using the claw position, cut across to the root for chopped onion.

HOW TO PEEL VEGETABLES

1 Place the vegetable on a chopping board and hold firmly at one end.

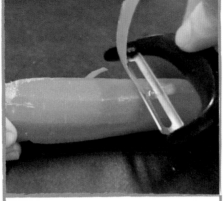

2 Starting three-quarters of the way from the top, run the peeler along the length of the vegetable, pressing down gently.

3 Keep turning to peel all the way around. Flip it around the other way to peel the remaining flesh at the top.

HOW TO USE A GRATER

1 Place the grater on a chopping board and hold with one hand. Hold the food with the other hand and at an angle.

2 Rub the food up and down the grater. Do not grate your knuckles or fingers!

A FUN WAY TO SEPARATE AN EGG

1 Crack an egg into a shallow bowl.

2 Take a clean empty plastic drink bottle. Squeeze the sides and put the opening up against the yolk. Release the sides and the yolk will be sucked in!

HOW TO AVOID A CRISIS

* Don't start cooking without asking an adult first. Ever.

* Wash your hands before you start cooking. Always.

* Wear an apron and tie your hair back if it's long. Finding hair in your food is a bit revolting.

* Make sure there's an adult nearby when you're cooking and always ask for help if you need it. Don't be shy!

* If you're not comfortable chopping, just grate things like onions and carrots instead. Simple.

* To stop a chopping board slipping when you're chopping, put a damp cloth underneath to keep it steady.

* Always wear oven gloves when you're putting things in and getting them out of the oven.

* Turn the pan handles to the side when they're on the hob so no one knocks into them. But don't turn them so that they sit over another hot hob!

* Always scrub your chopping board with warm water and washing up liquid after you've had raw meat, fish, chicken or eggs on it. Nasty bugs could make you sick.

HOW TO COOK
PERFECT PASTA

Soggy overcooked pasta is pretty awful. Follow these steps and you'll get it right every time. P.S. This is for dried pasta not fresh!

1 Work out how much pasta you need – about 100g (3½oz) per person is right, or a bit more for super-hungry adults.

2 Fill a very large pan with water – 1 litre (4 cups) per person is about right.

3 Carefully carry the pan to the hob – you might need an adult to help you.

ADULT HELP ALERT!

4 Add 1 teaspoon of fine sea salt for every person you're cooking for.

5 Turn the heat to high and wait for the water to boil fiercely – the bubbles should rise up the sides a bit.

6 Carefully add the pasta. If using long pasta like spaghetti, gently push it into the water with a wooden spoon.

7 Read the packet instructions and set the timer for 1 minute less than the cooking time. If it says 8–10 minutes, set it for 7.

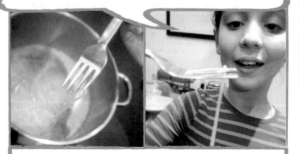

8 When the timer goes off, turn off the heat and very carefully take out a piece of pasta with a fork. When it's cool, bite into it. It should be soft but still a bit firm in the centre.

Serve immediate with your favourit sauce.

9 Drain the pasta into a colander. Shake it gently but don't shake off all the water. This will help to prevent it from drying out.

HOW TO COOK
PERFECT WHITE RICE

1 Measure the rice in a 250ml measuring cup rather than by weight. The proportion of rice to water will then be just right.

4 Cover the rice with cold water. Swish it around with your hand – the water will go milky.

2 One cup of uncooked rice will feed four people (if you're adding lots of other ingredients too!).

3 Measure your rice into a pan that has a lid, ideally one with a little hole to let out the excess steam.

5 Drain the rice in a sieve and tip back into the pan. Now add double the amount of water to rice (if you put in 1 cup of rice, add 2 cups of water).

Don't take the lid off during this time!

7 When done, turn off the heat and let sit for 5 minutes with the lid on. This makes the rice fluffy. Take the lid off: the rice should have absorbed all of the water.

Serve straight away with your favourite dish!

6 Set over a high heat. When it starts to boil and there are lots of bubbles, immediately turn the heat to low and put the lid on. Set your timer for 15 minutes.

2

MORNING MUNCHIES

FRUITY RICE PUFFS

" We reckon a lot of breakfast cereals are a bit boring, but not this. It's tasty, crispy and full of delicious fruit. Some cold milk is all you need. Let the person who does the shopping know that brown puffed rice is available to buy from health food shops. "

1 Set the oven to 180°C/380°F/Gas Mark 4.

3 Add the puffed rice and coconut to the bowl and mix. Set aside.

2 If you're using apricots, carefully chop them into small pieces. Put the fruit into a large mixing bowl.

TOP TIP

Dip your spoon in warm water before scooping out honey and it will come off more easily.

4 Put the butter and cinnamon in a small pan and set it over a medium heat.

5 Now add the honey.

Be careful as the mixture will get very hot as it melts.

6 Stir until the butter melts and the mixture starts to bubble.

It will smell cinnamazing!

8 Tip the puffs into a baking tray and gently spread them out with the back of a spoon.

7 Carefully pour the buttery mixture over the rice puffs, coconut and fruit mixture. Stir so all the puffs are covered in the sweet goo.

9 Wearing oven gloves, carefully put the baking tray in the oven and set the timer for 5 minutes.

Ask an adult to help if you like.

10 When the timer goes off, take the baking tray out and stir the puffs. Return the tray to the oven and set the timer for 2 minutes more.

11 Take the puffs out of the oven and let them cool in the tray. They'll crisp up as they cool.

Enjoy for breakfast! Or it's even pretty good as a snack.

NO RECIPE PANCAKES

> **This is so easy it's not really even a recipe – all you have to remember is 1, 1 and 1. We used a 250ml measuring cup but you could use one that's slightly smaller or larger – just use the same cup to measure out the milk and flour.**

YOU NEED

* 1 cup self-raising (self-rising) or plain (all-purpose) flour (self-raising flour makes fluffier pancakes)

* 1 cup milk

* 1 egg

* ½ tablespoon butter, for brushing

< **MAKES** about 20 >

1 To make the batter, mix the flour, milk and egg together in a bowl.

2 This doesn't look great to begin with, so time to get out a whisk to get rid of those lumps. Whisk until it is nice and smooth.

3 Melt the butter in a small pan over a medium heat and then take the pan off the heat.

4 Set a heavy frying pan over a high heat. Brush with some of the melted butter.

I'm like Van Gogh – but in the kitchen!

5 When the pan is very hot it will start to smoke a little. You should be able to hold your hand above it (without touching) and feel the heat. Now turn down the heat to medium.

6 Using a dessertspoon, dollop blobs of batter into the pan. We fit about 4 in ours. Don't worry if they are uneven. Be careful not to accidently touch the pan with your hands.

TOP TIP
Press down on the fish slice to get under each pancake.

Turn the heat down a little if the pan starts to smoke.

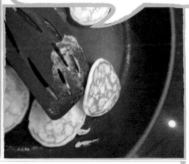

8 The pancakes will barely need any time at all to cook on the second side. Check to see if they're golden.

7 Cook until little bubbles start to form on the top. Carefully use a fish slice to turn the pancakes over.

VARIATIONS

Add ½ grated apple, ½ grated pear or a handful of berries to the batter and cook in the same way.

9 Slide them onto a plate and cover loosely with foil while you cook the rest.

10 Serve with honey or syrup, with some fruit on the side.

PAPER BAG BREAKFAST

This is great to cook when you're camping or on the barbecue at home when the sun is shining. It's VERY, VERY important to have an adult nearby when you're doing this. Make sure the fire has died down, otherwise the bag will just burn!

Ask the person who does the shopping to buy some greaseproof paper bags or brown paper sandwich bags.

1 Carefully cut the bacon rasher in half.

I am so hungry... I can't wait to eat this!

2 Butter the bread.

3 Cut a hole in the middle of the bread with a glass or a round cookie cutter.

TOP TIP

You can also cook this just as easily in the oven. Preheat the oven to 200°C/400°F/Gas Mark 6. Place your paper bag breakfast on a baking sheet instead of the barbecue and cook for 12–15 minutes.

4 Place both halves of the bacon in the middle of a largish piece of baking paper.

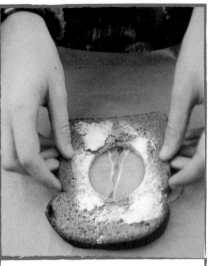

5 Put the bread on top, buttered-side up.

6 Taking your time, crack the egg into the hole. Aim precisely!

I have wrapped the bread up like a present!

7 Put the bread circle on top of the egg.

8 Neatly wrap the bread in the baking paper and carefully slide into a sandwich bag.

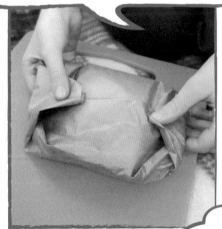

9 Carefully put on the barbecue. It will take about 5–10 minutes, so when you smell the bacon cooking, it's probably ready. Very carefully take them off the grill and check the egg is cooked.

ADULT HELP ALERT!

10 Open up the bag and unwrap your breakfast. No plate required! Perfect with lashings of ketchup.

CHOCOLATE CROISSANTS

66 **Just look at how easy these are to make! Just a bit of cutting and rolling. You can use either dark or milk chocolate or just roll up the pastry without a filling and spread with butter and jam when cooked.** 99

YOU NEED

* About 100g (3½oz) dark or milk chocolate
* 1 sheet ready-rolled puff pastry
* 1 egg
* Berries or fruit, to serve

< MAKES 8 >

1 Set the oven to 200°C/400°F/ Gas Mark 6.

2 Line a baking sheet with a piece of baking paper.

3 Break the chocolate into small pieces. Try to make them long and thin.

It won't matter if I eat a sneaky piece, surely?!

4 Unroll the pastry onto a chopping board. Using a sharp knife, carefully cut the pastry into quarters.

5 Cut each quarter diagonally into 2 triangles.

20

6 Put some chocolate along one of the short edges of the triangle. Roll up the pastry, aiming towards the opposite pointy end. Gently press the point so that it stays in place.

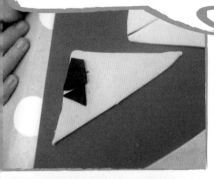

Keep rolling, rolling, rolling...

8 Crack the egg into a small bowl and whisk with a fork.

7 Lightly pinch the pastry together at the ends and bend them inwards to make a half-moon shape. Place them on the baking sheet as you go.

9 Lightly brush the croissants with the egg.

11 They should be crisp and golden. Sometimes they end up in funny shapes because they unwrap slightly – don't worry, they still taste brilliant!

Eat warm with some fruit on the side.

10 Wearing oven gloves, carefully slide the baking sheet into the oven. Set the timer for 15 minutes.

Watch out for croissant thieves!

CHOCOLATE AND BANANA FRENCH TOAST

" This is so yum. Make it for your adults and you'll definitely earn some brownie points. It's a bit of a treat, and definitely not for breakfast every day! "

1 Set the oven to 200°C/400°F/Gas Mark 6.

2 Line a baking sheet with baking paper.

3 To break the chocolate, place it in a plastic bag and bash it with a rolling pin – make sure you leave some biggish bits. Tip into a bowl.

4 Slice the banana and add to the bowl with the chocolate.

I think we should taste it in case it's poisonous...

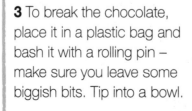

5 Mash together with a fork.

22

Make a second sandwich the same way.

8 Crack the eggs into a shallow bowl. A soup plate is perfect. Add the milk, vanilla, sugar and melted butter and whisk.

6 Spread half the mashed banana on a slice of bread. Press another piece of bread on top and cut in half.

7 Place the butter in a small pan and melt it over a medium heat. Set aside.

11 Wearing oven gloves, slide the sheet into the oven and set the timer for 8 minutes.

They're really slimy but will taste fantastic!

It should be golden underneath.

12 Wearing gloves, take the baking sheet out of the oven and very carefully flip the toast over with a fish slice.

9 Dip the sandwiches into the eggy mixture, turning them so they're completely soaked.

10 Place the gooey bread onto the baking sheet as you go.

Be careful – it's delicious but very hot!

13 Return the toast to the oven and set the timer for another 8 minutes.

14 When the timer goes off, take the tray out of the oven and let it sit for a few minutes before you tuck in.

BOILED EGGS AND DIPPY THINGS

To get your eggs lovely and soft for dipping you need a timer or they might not turn out eggsactly right! The timings here are for eggs that have NOT been sitting in the fridge. If you are using cold eggs or a large pan, add another 30 seconds to the cooking time.

DIPPY THINGS

* **Soldiers**: Just butter is brilliant but we also like soldiers spread with squished avocado or pesto. You can even try honey dippers!

* **Asparagus**: While the eggs are cooking, bring a pan of water to the boil and very carefully add the asparagus. Boil for about 3 minutes, then drain and run under cold water.

* **Breadsticks wrapped in ham**: Spread some ham with a little mayonnaise and wrap it around a breadstick. Delish.

* **Chips (fries)**: This is definitely not for breakfast! Cook the Cheat's Chips on pages 42–43 first.

I'm looking a bit tired this morning! Maybe an egg will wake me up!

1 Use the smallest pan that will fit the number of eggs you're cooking. If they fit snuggly they won't clatter around and crack. Place the eggs in the pan and cover with cold water.

2 Set the pan over a high heat and bring the water to the boil. What you are looking for is nice big bubbles, not tiny fizzy drink bubbles.

3 As soon as the water starts to boil, turn off the heat and cover with a lid.

Be very careful when carrying a hot pan.

Cut off the tops and dunk with you dippy things!

4 Quickly set the timer for 5 minutes. This will make eggs with a runny yolk and a set white – perfect for dipping.

5 It's a good idea to start cooking your toast now, or make one of the other dippy suggestions above.

6 When the timer goes off, safely carry your pan to the sink and run cold water over the eggs. This stops them from cooking. Use a spoon to lift them into egg cups.

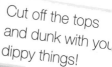

SENSATIONAL SMOOTHIE

" We think this is the tastiest way in the world to "eat" fruit and it's great fun to make. Experiment by using your favourite fruit but try to keep banana in it as it makes the smoothie thick and creamy. "

YOU NEED

* 1 large ripe banana

* 100g (3½oz) strawberries

* 150g (5½oz) pineapple pieces (ripe and fresh or from a can)

* 125ml (½ cup) pineapple or apple juice, or more if you like your smoothie less thick

* 2 tablespoons coconut milk or natural yoghurt (optional)

< SERVES 2 >

TOP TIP
You can freeze the banana for a couple of hours if you want your smoothie to be ice cold.

WARNING!
Be careful not to put your fingers near the blade.

2 Using the claw method on page 8, cut the green tops off the strawberries and then in half. Add them to the processor.

3 Tip in the pineapple and the juice.

1 Peel the banana, break it into pieces and place them into a food processor.

4 If you're using it, add the coconut milk or yoghurt.

5 Blitz until the smoothie is, well, smooth!

ADULT HELP ALERT!

VARIATIONS

* Add 2–3 tablespoons of breakfast cereal.

* Add a little maple syrup, golden syrup or honey.

* You could add mango, blueberries, pears, kiwi fruit, raspberries, watermelon, peaches, a squeeze of lime or lemon juice or a little grated ginger.

3

SCRUMMY BASICS

MAGIC
SAUCE

"With some simple cooking hocus pocus you can transform this basic sauce into other really delicious pasta or chicken dishes. You can even turn it into soup!"

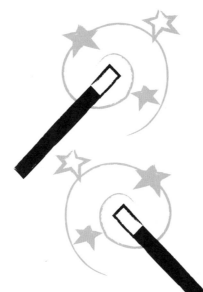

YOU NEED

* ½ onion
* 1 garlic clove
* 1 tablespoon olive oil
* 1 x 400g (14oz) tin (can) chopped tomatoes
* A big pinch of sugar

< SERVES 2–4 with pasta >

1 Finely chop the onion following the instructions on page 8.

2 Crush the garlic clove by squashing it lightly under a bowl. Peel off the skin.

3 Heat the oil in a pan, set over a medium heat and very carefully add the onion.

4 Stir with a wooden spoon and then turn down the heat to medium-low. Cook for 7 minutes, stirring now and then.

TOP TIP Put a small piece of onion in first to test if the oil is hot enough. If it makes a gentle sizzling noise, it's perfect. If the oil spits, turn down the heat and wait a minute or so before adding the onion. If it doesn't make any noise, let the oil heat up a bit more and test again.

A bit of kitchen dancing and singing is fun while you wait – but do it away from the stove!

5 The onion should be soft, squishy and a little bit clear – what cookbooks call "translucent".

7 When it starts to bubble turn the heat down to low and put the lid on. Set the timer for 30 minutes.

6 Add the tomatoes, the flattened garlic clove and the sugar. Stir.

8 Stir every now and then, and use a masher to squash the tomatoes. When the timer goes off, the sauce should be thick and smell wonderful.

Or use it on the pizza bases on pages 46–47.

9 This sauce is fantastico with pasta – see page 10 for how to cook pasta perfectly.

VARIATIONS

BEST TOMATO SOUP

1 Let the sauce cool a bit then carefully tip it into a strainer resting over a bowl. Push the sauce through with a wooden spoon. Scrape in any thick bits on the bottom of the sieve. Tip the soup back into the pan and warm it up over a medium-low heat. If it's too thick for your taste, add a little milk. Fry some chopped chorizo in a little oil and sprinkle this on top of the soup if you like.

SAUCY DIPPERS

1 Spoon some sauce over the chicken dippers on page 41. Sprinkle with cheese and cook in the oven. Seriously yum.

ITALIAN SAUCE

1 Fry some chopped bacon with the onion and add a pinch of chilli flakes with the tomatoes for a spicy, meaty sauce.

2 Add torn up basil leaves, black olives and chopped canned anchovies to the sauce 10 minutes before the end of cooking. Don't worry: the anchovies melt down and you won't even taste them!

BANGERS AND MASH

> All our mates love sausages and mashed potato, and so do we. The bangers cook in the oven which means you can get on with the mash. Easy peasy.

YOU NEED

* 8 sausages
* 6 large potatoes
* 150ml (⅔ cup) milk
* 50g (2oz) butter

< SERVES 4 >

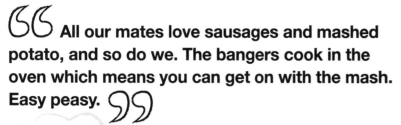

1 Set the oven to 190°C/380°F/Gas Mark 5.

CAREFUL – it's heavy!

2 Put the sausages in a baking tray. Snip them apart with kitchen scissors or a knife if they're joined.

3 Wear oven gloves. Carefully slide the tray into the oven and set the timer for 30 minutes.

4 Now, half fill a large pan with cold water.

 SHORTCUT! We love mashed potatoes with the skin on, so you can skip peeling them if you want to.

5 Very carefully peel the potatoes using the method on page 9.

Make sure the potatoes are completely covered by the water.

6 Cut the potatoes in half and place into the pan of water.

Keep an eye on the pan and turn the heat down if it looks like it's going to boil over.

7 Set the pan over a high heat and bring the water to the boil. Turn down to medium. Set the timer for 15 minutes.

8 When the potato timer goes off, check to see if they are done by sticking a skewer into one. If it slides in easily, they are cooked.

ADULT HELP ALERT!

9 Drain the potatoes in a colander and tip them into a large bowl. Cover with the pan lid to keep warm.

10 Put the milk and butter into a small pan, set it over a medium heat and cook until the butter has melted.

11 Pour the milk mixture over the potatoes.

12 Mash with a masher until the potatoes are nice and creamy. Cover the bowl with the pan lid to help keep the mash warm.

ADULT HELP ALERT!

13 The sausages should be golden when done. Use oven gloves to remove them from the oven.

14 Spoon some mash onto each plate and top with 2 sausages.

Eat with big blobs of tomato ketchup!

SHORT CUT LASAGNE

YOU NEED

* 120g (4¼oz) Cheddar cheese or similar
* 120g (4¼oz) mozzarella
* 350ml (1½ cups) crème fraîche
* A pinch of nutmeg
* 1 quantity Bolognese sauce (see pages 36–37)
* About 9 lasagne sheets

< SERVES 4–6 >

66 **Everyone loves lasagne! It's not really cheating to make it this way – it's just a quick and easy version because there's no complicated white sauce.** 99

TOP TIP
It's easier to make the lasagne when the Bolognese sauce is hot.

1 Set the oven to 180°C/350°F/Gas Mark 4. Carefully grate both cheeses (see page 9) and set aside.

2 Pour the crème fraîche into a pan and set it over a medium heat.

3 Add most of the grated Cheddar and mozzarella, but leave 1 handful of each aside. You'll need this to sprinkle over the top before it goes in the oven.

4 Add the nutmeg and stir, stir, stir! You want the crème fraîche and cheese to melt together – once it's oozy turn off the heat.

5 Now you need to put together the lasagne. Ladle some of the Bolognese into an ovenproof dish. We used one about 18 x 28cm (7 x 11in) but it doesn't have to be exact. Spread it out with the back of a spoon to make a thin layer.

6 Place a single layer of lasagne sheets on top – try not to overlap them. You might have to snap some into smaller pieces to fit.

7 Spoon over some of the white sauce and spread it out right to the edges. It will be lovely and stringy so try not to gloop it everywhere.

Ewww! It looks like a spider's web!

8 Now add another layer of Bolognese, then lasagne sheets and cheese sauce. Repeat until you've almost reached the top.

TOP TIP
Thin layers are better as they will cook much more easily.

9 Finish with a layer of cheese sauce and sprinkle with the rest of the two types of grated cheese.

ADULT HELP ALERT!

Use oven gloves or get help when taking the dish out of the oven.

10 Slide the dish into the oven (*oops! we forgot to put on oven gloves!*) Set the timer for 30 minutes. It is ready when golden on top and bubbling at the edges.

11 Gobble down with your favourite veggies.

CHINESE FRIED RICE

66 **There's a little bit of chopping to do here but otherwise it's pretty simple and super scrumptious. With the prawns it is a really tasty and filling dinner.** 99

YOU NEED

* 185g (about 1 cup) white rice
* 1 small piece of ginger, about 2cm (1in) long
* 2 garlic cloves
* 3 spring onions (scallions)
* 2 slices of ham
* ½ red pepper
* 2 eggs
* 1 tablespoon vegetable oil
* 3 tablespoons sweetcorn (frozen or from a can)
* 3 tablespoons frozen peas
* 150g (5½oz) cooked prawns (shrimp) (optional)
* 3 tablespoons soy sauce
* ½ teaspoon sesame oil (optional)

< **SERVES** 4–6 >

1 Cook the rice following the instructions on page 11. Set aside.

2 While the rice is cooking, start your chopping! Carefully peel the ginger and finely grate it. Transfer to a small bowl.

3 Peel the garlic and crush it into the bowl using a garlic press.

4 Using the method on page 8, cut the hairy ends off the onions, remove any papery skin and finely slice. Place in the bowl.

5 Cut the ham and pepper into small pieces. Set aside.

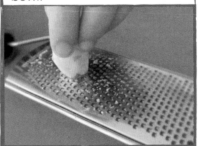

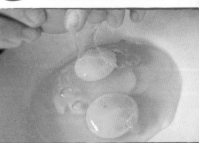

6 Crack the eggs into a bowl and whisk with a fork.

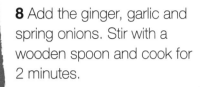

8 Add the ginger, garlic and spring onions. Stir with a wooden spoon and cook for 2 minutes.

It smells so delicious!

7 Heat the vegetable oil in a large frying pan over a medium heat.

The pan will be very full at this point so try not to get it everywhere as you stir!

9 Add the ham, pepper, sweetcorn and peas. Cook, stirring often, for 4 minutes.

10 Add the rice, prawns (if using), soy sauce and eggs. Stir and cook for 2 minutes.

Serve with a little drizzle of sesame oil if you like.

11 Stirring will ensure it is all warmed through.

BOLOGNESE SAUCE

Bolognese is possibly the best pasta sauce ever invented and this version is deliciously simple. You can also use it to make other things like lasagne (pages 32–33), baked potatoes (pages 54–55) or cottage pie.

YOU NEED

* 1 onion
* 1 carrot
* 1 garlic clove
* 2 tablespoons olive oil
* 400g (14oz) minced (ground) beef
* 450ml (2 cups) passata
* 400ml (2 cups) water
* 1 bay leaf
* 1 teaspoon dried oregano
* 1 beef or vegetable stock (bouillon) cube

< **SERVES** 4–6 with pasta >

TOP TIP If you don't like chopping, grate the vegetables instead.

1 Finely chop the onion and the carrot using the method on pages 8–9.

2 Peel the garlic, cut the clove in half if it is large and crush in a garlic press. Set aside in a bowl.

WARNING! Be careful as the hot oil can spit.

3 Heat 1 tablespoon of the oil in a large pan over a medium heat. Very carefully add the onion and carrot and stir so everything is coated in oil.

4 Turn the heat to low and cook for about 7 minutes, stirring every now and then. It's important to cook the veg like this as slow cooking makes it soft and sweet.

If you add the garlic before this it's likely burn.

5 Stir in the garlic. Cook for 3 minutes.

6 Scoop the vegetables out of the pan and put them aside in a bowl.

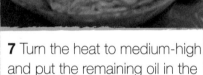

WARNING!
Watch out for spitting oil.

7 Turn the heat to medium-high and put the remaining oil in the pan. Add the meat.

...e these dark brown ...s? That's where all ...e flavour's hiding.

8 Break up the mince with a spoon. Leave it to cook for 3 minutes without stirring. This way it will go nice and brown underneath.

9 Add the onion and carrot to the pan and mix together. Add the passata, water, bay leaf and oregano.

11 If you're having pasta (page 10), start cooking it just before the sauce has finished cooking.

10 Crumble in the stock cube and stir. When it is ...ubbling, turn down to low. Simmer ...tly – small bubbles – for 30 minutes. ...ir now and then. The sauce should be thick, dark brown and full of flavour.

VARIATIONS
CHILLI

1 Follow all of the instructions for the Bolognese, but at step 9, as you add the passata, also add in a drained **400g (14oz) tin (can) of kidney beans, 1 teaspoon of ground cumin, 1 teaspoon of chilli powder** and **1 teaspoon of sweet paprika**. This chilli is delicious with rice (page 11) or on top of a baked potato (pages 54–55).

COTTAGE PIE

1 Make a batch of the mashed potato on pages 30–31. Set the oven to 180°C/350°F/Gas Mark 4.

2 Very carefully tip the Bolognese into a shallow ovenproof dish. Ask an adult to help you with this. We used an 18 x 28cm (7 x 11in) dish.

ADULT HELP ALERT!

3 Spoon the mashed potato over the Bolognese and smooth it with the back of a spoon. Dot pieces of butter over the top of the potato.

4 Carefully transfer the dish to the oven and bake for 25–30 minutes. The potato topping should be golden and the sauce should be bubbling. Ask an adult to take it out of the oven as it will be very hot.

MAC 'N' CHEESE

" Gooey and delicious, this is the best macaroni and cheese ever. We like peas and ham in ours, but you can leave them out if you want to. This is lovely served with some crisp veggies on the side. "

YOU NEED

* 300g (10½oz) macaroni or other pasta shapes
* 100g (3½oz) Parmesan cheese
* 200g (7oz) Cheddar cheese
* 100g (3½oz) ham
* 2 tablespoons plain (all-purpose) flour
* 500ml (2 cups) milk
* 100g (⅔ cup) frozen peas
* 4 tablespoons dried breadcrumbs

< SERVES 4–6 >

ADULT HELP ALERT!

1 Cook the macaroni by following the instructions for cooking pasta on page 10.

This will stop the pasta sticking together.

2 When the macaroni is draining in the colander, run it under cold water and shake. Tip it back into the pan and set aside.

BE CAREFUL We don't want grated finger!

3 Using the method on page 9, grate both cheeses, using the largest holes on the grater.

4 Mix the cheeses together. Put a large handful aside and save this to sprinkle over the macaroni just before it goes in the oven.

You will need to stop thieves from stealing the cheese!

5 Cut the ham into small pieces.

6 Set the oven to 190°C/380°F/ Gas Mark 5.

7 Put the flour in a small bowl. Pour in about 200ml (¾ cup) of the milk and whisk until there are no lumps.

8 Pour the rest of the milk into a small pan and set over a medium heat. When steam starts to rise and there are little bubbles at the edges of the pan, pour in the milk and flour mixture.

The sauce is ready when it looks like thick cream.

9 Stir without stopping for 4 minutes. It should only bubble very gently, so you might need to lower the heat. Just keep stirring!

11 Add the ham and peas and set over a medium heat. Keep stirring until all the cheese has melted. The sauce should be gloopy and smell scrummy.

10 Take the pan off the heat and add the cheese (except for the cheese you set aside).

CAREFUL It's superdooper hot.

It sounds like squelchy mud!

12 Carefully pour the sauce into the pan of pasta and stir. Tip into a shallow ovenproof dish.

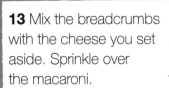

13 Mix the breadcrumbs with the cheese you set aside. Sprinkle over the macaroni.

14 Using oven gloves, place the dish in the oven and cook for about 20 minutes. When it's done, the sauce should be bubbling and the top golden.

ADULT HELP ALERT!

15 Wearing oven gloves, carefully take the dish out of the oven and let it sit for 5 minutes before serving.

FABULOSO

FISH FINGERS

" These go brilliantly with the chips (fries) on pages 42–43. Prepare the chips first and while they're in the oven, start cooking your fish. If the chips finish first just cover them loosely with foil until you're ready. "

YOU NEED

* 80g (¾ cup) dried breadcrumbs
* 50g (½ cup) flour
* 2 eggs
* 500g (1lb 2oz) white skinless fish fillets, such as cod, gurnard, haddock or pollock

< SERVES 4 very hungry people or 6 small people **>**

1 Set the oven to 200°C/ 400°F/Gas Mark 6. Line a baking sheet with baking paper.

2 Spread the breadcrumbs out on a dinner plate or in a shallow bowl.

3 Spread the flour out on another plate.

4 Crack the eggs into a shallow bowl and whisk with a fork.

5 Cut the fish into neat pieces. Slice the fillets lengthways and then cut each strip into fish finger-size pieces. Try to get them all about the same size.

 Ask the person who does the shopping to see if they can find panko breadcrumbs – they're Japanese-style breadcrumbs that will make the fingers extra crunchy. Or you can use crushed cornflakes!

6 Now for the gloopy bit. Dip each piece of fish into the flour and turn it over so it's coated.

7 Dip it into the egg.

It feels super-slimy!

8 Cover in breadcrumbs. Gently press to stick. Place the crumbed fish on to the baking sheet.

Aarrgh! Monster hands!

9 Wearing oven gloves, slide the baking sheet into the oven and set your timer for 10 minutes.

WARNING! Don't wander off – keep an eye on them so that they don't burn.

10 Your fish fingers should be lovely and golden when done. Eat them while they're hot with chips (fries), peas, mayonnaise and a squeeze of lemon juice.

VARIATION

CHICKEN NUGGET DIPPERS

Use 4 skinless chicken breasts instead of the fish.

1 Cut the chicken into strips about 2.5cm (1in) wide and then cut into bite-size pieces.

2 Crumb the chicken in the same way as the fish and place on a lined baking sheet. Cook for about 18 minutes at 200°C/400°F/Gas Mark 6. Check if the chicken is cooked by cutting open a nugget – the meat should be white. If it's at all pink, pop it back into the oven for a few more minutes. Check again.

3 Eat with guacamole (pages 110–111) and ketchup.

CHEAT'S
CHIPS

" These chips (fries) are so tasty you could pretend they're deep fried (they're actually cooked in the oven). Add some flavourings if you like – we love cheese – and serve them with the fish fingers on pages 40–41 or whatever else you fancy for dinner. "

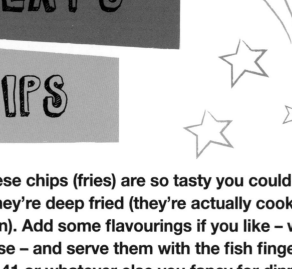

1 Using the method on page 8, cut the potatoes in half lengthways. Place cut-side down on your chopping board and slice in half again. Slice each piece into three or four chips.

VERY IMPORTANT NOTICE!

We think keeping the skin on the potatoes makes the chips even tastier, but if you want to peel them follow the instructions on page 9.

3 Tip the chips into a bowl and carefully cover with hot tap water. Set the bowl aside for 10 minutes.

2 Put the chips in a colander and rinse really well under cold water. This will wash off some of the starch and help them to crisp up.

4 Set the oven to 230°C/450°F/Gas Mark 8.

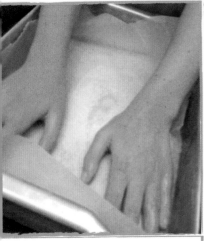

6 Drain the chips into a colander. Spread some paper towel on your work surface and tip out the chips. Pat them dry.

5 Cut out a piece of baking paper and use it to line a baking tray.

7 Put the chips into a large bowl and add the olive oil. If you're using any of the flavourings (apart from the cheese) add them now. Mix with your hands!

8 Spread them out on your baking tray so they don't touch each other. Place in the oven and set the timer for 15 minutes.

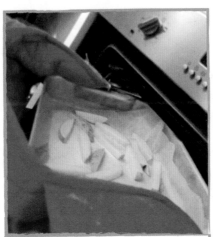

10 If you're making cheesy chips, sprinkle with cheese now. Return the tray to the oven and set the timer for another 15 minutes.

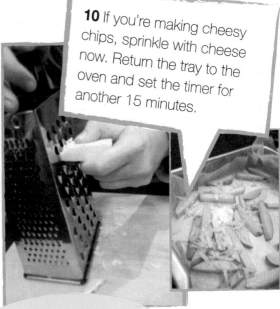

9 Using oven gloves, carefully take the tray out of the oven and turn the chips over with a fish slice.

TOP TIP
If your chips are cooked before the other things you're eating, switch off the oven and leave the door open a little. This way they'll stay nice and warm.

11 When done they should be golden, cooked through and very enticing!

4

WHEN MATES COME OVER

EASY PEASY PIZZA

This is really fun to make when mates come over. Everyone can help with the dough and then each person can add whatever toppings they like. We all love ham and pineapple – Italians say it's not traditional, but we don't care! You need to start this recipe by making the dough on pages 102–103.

recipe by making the dough on pages 102–103.

YOU NEED

* 1 quantity of dough (the recipe is on pages 102–103)

* Flour, for sprinkling

* 250ml (generous 1 cup) passata

* Whatever toppings you like, for example:
  Ham and pineapple
  Salami
  Fresh tomato and basil
  Tuna and sweetcorn
  Sliced red pepper

* 500g (5 cups) grated mozzarella

< **MAKES** 4 big pizzas >

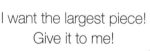

I want the largest piece! Give it to me!

1 Set the oven to 200°C/400°F/Gas Mark 6. Take the dough ball and cut it into 4 equal pieces.

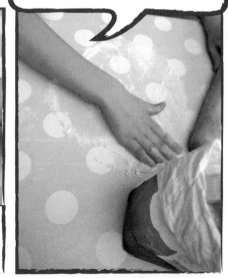

2 Sprinkle some flour on a clean work surface. Spread it out as you will need to roll your pizza base quite big.

3 Take a piece of dough and place it in the middle.

4 Gently press down on the dough with your rolling pin and push it away from you, then bring the rolling pin back to the centre and roll it towards you.

Sprinkle over a bit more flour if it gets sticky.

5 Flip the dough over every now and then, and turn it sideways, so that you roll the dough into a circle.

6 Roll the dough as thin as possible. A big circle is great but some people want their pizza in weird shapes. That's fine.

Add the passata right up to the edge of the pizza.

7 Slide the dough onto sheets of baking paper.

8 Add a blob of passata to the base and smooth it out with the back of a spoon.

9 Add your chosen toppings and generously sprinkle with mozzarella.

TOP TIP You might have to cook these pizzas 1 or 2 at a time. Just share them while you wait – don't worry, they don't take long!

12 Very carefully take the pizzas out and cut into pieces. Watch it! They are really hot.

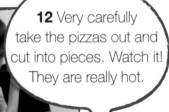

ADULT HELP ALERT!

10 Slide the sheet of baking paper onto a baking sheet and using oven gloves, put the pizzas into the oven.

11 Set the timer for 8 minutes. When done the cheese should be melted and the base golden. If it's not quite ready, cook for 2 more minutes.

BRILLIANT BURGERS WITH EVERYTHING

" The apple in these burgers makes them extra juicy. We've cooked them on the barbecue, but it's not a problem if you want to cook them in a frying pan or a griddle. "

1 Put the mince in a large bowl and squish it up a bit with your hands.

Go on, get in there, it's not going to bite you!

2 Following the instructions on pages 8–9, cut the onion in half. Remove the skin and carefully grate each half.

CAUTION
You don't want a grated finger burger!

3 Now grate the apple, turning it as you go, until only the core is left.

4 Add the grated onion, grated apple, breadcrumbs, dried herbs, tomato ketchup and barbecue or Worcestershire sauce to the meat. Mix it all together with your hands.

Yep, it's really gooey!

5 Crack the egg into the bowl and mix until everything is combined.

6 Make a ball the size of a small apple and flatten it into a burger shape. Repeat with the rest of the mixture.

7 These are great cooked on a barbecue but a hot frying pan or griddle works as well.

ADULT HELP ALERT!

8 Cook for about 7 minutes, flipping the burgers over every minute or so to prevent them from burning.

IF YOU DO NOT HAVE A BBQ

If you are using a frying or griddle pan heat 1 tablespoon of olive oil over a medium heat and cook in batches, 4 burgers at a time.

Don't flip these ones!

9 If you're having cheesy burgers, place a slice of cheese on top of each burger about 2 minutes before the end of the cooking time.

10 Meanwhile, split the burger buns. Toast them in the toaster or under the grill (broiler) or eat them as they come. Add whatever you fancy to one half of the bun: tomato, lettuce, beetroot, pineapple or more sauce.

11 Add the cooked burger and pop the other half of the bun on top.

Seriously good and a bit messy!

TOASTY BASKETS

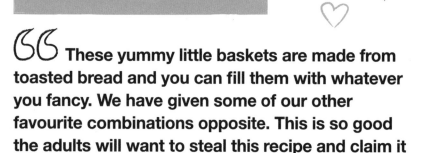

YOU NEED

* 8 slices of bread
* 30g (1oz) butter
* 4 good-quality sausages
* 100g (3½oz) Cheddar or your favourite cheese
* 1 teaspoon fennel seeds (optional)

< **MAKES** 8 baskets >

"" These yummy little baskets are made from toasted bread and you can fill them with whatever you fancy. We have given some of our other favourite combinations opposite. This is so good the adults will want to steal this recipe and claim it as their own! ""

1 Set the oven to 180°C/350°F/ Gas Mark 4.

3 Roll the slices out with a rolling pin until they are lovely and thin.

2 Very carefully cut the crusts off the bread. (Ask an adult if they want these to make breadcrumbs.)

4 Put the butter in a small pan and melt it over a medium heat.

5 Pour the butter into a little bowl. Brush both sides of the bread with the butter.

6 Gently press the bread into the holes of a large muffin tin. Press the overlapping bits flat so it forms a neat little basket.

Don't worry if you make a hole – just squish it back together.

7 Carefully trim the scraggly bits of bread around the top if you want the baskets to be super neat, but you don't need to do this.

8 Cut open the sausages and squeeze the meat into a bowl.

9 Carefully grate the cheese (see page 9) and add this to the bowl with the meat.

This smells gorgeous and it really adds a lot of flavour.

10 Put the fennel seeds into a mortar and crush with a pestle. If you don't have one of these, use a rolling pin to break up the seeds. Add to the sausage mixture.

11 Mix everything together with your hands.

12 Divide the sausage mixture between the bread baskets. Don't press down too firmly.

13 Wearing oven gloves, slide the tray into the oven and set the timer for 20 minutes. When done, the sausage should be bubbling and the baskets golden.

14 Leave the baskets in the muffin tin for a couple of minutes before tucking in!

OUR FAVE FILLINGS

HOT

* TUNA & SWEETCORN
Mix 1 small can of tuna, 60g (2oz) grated cheese, 4 tablespoons of sweetcorn and 4 tablespoons of sour cream or crème fraîche.

* EGG Whisk 4 raw eggs and mix with at least 6 tablespoons of grated cheese.

COLD

Bake the empty baskets for 10–15 minutes or until golden and fill with:

* GUACAMOLE Pages 110–111.

* CHEESE & TOMATO Grate or tear a large ball of mozzarella and mix with 4 chopped tomatoes.

* SALMON & CREAM CHEESE
Chop 6 smoked salmon strips and mix with 4 tablespoons of cream cheese.

DIY FISH PARCELS

" Some of our friends didn't like fish until they tasted it cooked this way. You might think some of these concoctions sound a bit weird, but they're really delicious and simple. And the smell is fantastic when everyone opens their own parcel. "

1 Set the oven to 200°C/ 400°F/Gas Mark 6.

2 Tear off a large piece of tin foil – it has to be big enough to easily wrap your fish loosely.

What shall I put on top of mine? Decisions, decisions!

3 Place your chosen piece of fish in the middle of the foil, with the skin-side down.

TASTE ALERT

If you want to experiment with your own favourite ingredients just make sure any vegetables are cut small or grated and you add a splash of liquid (like milk or water). That's it!

4 Make it into a basic open box shape by folding up the sides.

5 Place your chosen ingredients on top of the fish.

6 Scrunch the foil to make a parcel but don't wrap it tight like a present! There needs to be plenty of air inside for the fish to steam.

Don't forget which one is yours – they all look the same when wrapped!

7 Place them in a baking tray. Wearing oven gloves, slide the tray into the oven and set the timer for 20 minutes.

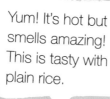

Yum! It's hot but smells amazing! This is tasty with plain rice.

8 Very carefully serve everyone their parcel on a plate and let them slowly open it themselves.

VARIATIONS

JAMMY FISH

This is a great recipe for people who think that they don't like fish.

* 1 or 2 teaspoons apricot jam (jelly)
* 1 garlic clove, peeled and crushed
* ½ tablespoon butter
* A small splash of soy sauce
* A small splash of milk

MILD CURRY

* 2 tablespoons coconut milk
* 1 teaspoon green curry paste (or more if you like spicy food)
* ½ tablespoon soy sauce
* 2 or 3 tablespoons grated courgettes (zucchinis)
* A splash of fish sauce (optional)
* A few drops of sesame oil (optional)

PERFECT PESTO

* 1 tablespoon pesto
* A small handful of grated carrot
* A handful of grated cheese
* A splash of milk

BAKED POTATOES WITH TOPPINGS

66 **We don't know anyone who doesn't like baked potatoes and they're perfect to cook when friends come over. We've suggested some tasty toppings to go with them – put these on the table and let everyone help themselves.** 99

4 Pour a little oil over each potato – you don't need very much. The oil will help to make the skins really crispy.

1 Set the oven to 200°C/400°F/ Gas Mark 6.

Be very careful not to stab your hands.

Some potatoes are enormous!

2 Wash the potatoes until clean. Dry them well.

3 Stab each potato with a fork a few times. This will stop them exploding in the oven!

Now, get mucky.

6 Sprinkle over a little salt – this will help to make the skin even more crispy.

5 Using your hands, rub the oil into the potatoes. Put them in a large baking tray.

8 Depending on the size of the potatoes, they will take between 1 hour – 1 hour 20 minutes to become golden and crispy on the outside and cooked through and fluffy in the middle.

10 Cut the potatoes down the middle, open them up and add your favourite topping.

7 Wearing oven gloves, place the baking tray into the oven.

9 To check if they're done, stick a skewer into the middle of the largest potato. If it slides through easily, they are cooked.

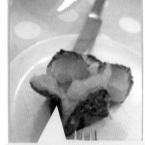

WARNING! These will be steaming hot!

OUR FAVE TOPPINGS

* **TUNA, SWEETCORN AND MAYONNAISE**
  Mix together 1 tin (can) of tuna, 1 small tin of sweetcorn and 2 tablespoons of mayonnaise.
* **GUACAMOLE** See pages 110–111.
* **CHOPPED HAM AND GRATED CHEESE**
* **COLESLAW**
* **CHILLI OR BOLOGNESE** See pages 36–37.
* **PESTO**
* **SOUR CREAM AND SMOKED SALMON**
  Chop a few strips of smoked salmon and mix with 3 tablespoons of sour cream.

KICK 'N' ROLL

TIN CAN

ICE CREAM

66 **This is genius – really simple and extremely good fun. All you need to do is put your ingredients in a tin, roll it and you will have instant ice cream!** 99

Try not to eat it all at this point!

1 Pour both creams into a jug and then add the sugar and the vanilla.

2 Give it a good stir.

3 Carefully pour the mixture into one of the zip-lock bags. Zip the bag securely and place it inside the second zip-lock bag. This is in case one of the bags gets torn when you're "churning" it. Gently put the bag of cream aside.

This is tricky so get someone to hold the bag for you.

You're right – it doesn't look very yummy yet, but just you wait.

4 Place a thick layer of ice in the bottom of the tin. Sprinkle the ice with one-third of the rock salt.

5 Place the bag of cream on top of the ice. Pack some more ice around the bag and sprinkle half of the remaining salt over the top.

6 Fill the tin to the top with more ice and sprinkle over the rest of the salt.

It's a good idea to secure the lid with some tape.

7 Put the lid on the tin. Make sure it is tightly shut.

Now for the fun bit!

8 You need to roll the can around for about 25 minutes to "churn" it.

Don't forget to grab some spoons if you're heading to the park!

9 How you do this is up to you: roll it down a hill or along a footpath, or kick it along very gently. We used a skateboard ramp.

10 Once ready, take off the lid, remove the bag and ta dah! Gorgeous creamy ice cream. Mix in any extras.

TROUBLE SHOOTING

When you open the bag be careful not to let in any salt or the ice cream will taste disgusting. If it is not quite ready, give the bag a squidge with your hands, pop it back in the tin, add some fresh ice and salt, and roll it for 5 more minutes.

5

PUDDINGS AND YUMMIES TO SHARE

STRIPY
SUNDAES

66 This pudding looks really impressive and there's no cooking involved. Use your favourite fruits – we've listed some scrummy combos on the opposite page. You don't have to use fresh fruit – fruit from a can works really well, but drain away the juice in a sieve first. **99**

YOU NEED

* At least 2 different kinds of soft fruit (see suggestions on the opposite page), about 400g (14oz) in total

* 150g (5½ oz) chocolate biscuits (cookies) with icing (frosting) in the middle

* 200g (1 cup) cream cheese

* 160g (⅔ cup) plain yoghurt

* 1 teaspoon vanilla extract

< SERVES 4 >

TOP TIP If you're using banana, wait until you are ready to assemble your sundae to slice it or it will turn brown.

1 Carefully chop the fruit using the method on page 8. You want it quite small. Put each fruit into a separate bowl.

Be careful not to hurt your fingers!

2 Place the chocolate biscuits in a zip-lock freezer bag, seal and bash with a rolling pin.

3 When the crumbs are very fine tip them into a bowl.

Don't sneak too many tastes or there'll be none left!

4 Add 2 teaspoons of the cream cheese to the biscuit crumbs. Stir until the cheese is completely mixed in.

6 Now, it's time to get mucky and assemble the sundaes. Find 4 small glasses or jars.

5 Put the rest of the cream cheese, the yoghurt and the vanilla into a bowl and stir until smooth and creamy.

7 Sprinkle about 1 tablespoon (or more if you need it) of biscuit crumbs into each glass and press down with your fingers or a spoon.

Try to do it neatly so you don't mix in any biscuit crumbs.

10 Repeat the layers until you get to the top of the glass, finishing with cream and finally fruit.

8 Place a dollop of cream cheese mixture on top and lightly spread it out.

9 Add quite a thick a layer of chopped fruit.

Dig in!

SOME DELICIOUSLY FRUITY IDEAS

* Pineapple (fresh or canned) and banana
* Strawberries and blueberries
* Peaches (fresh or canned) and passion fruit
* Blackberries (fresh or canned) and apple

11 Put the sundaes in the fridge for about 30 minutes to chill and firm up.

SUPER SCRUMMY SURPRISE SORBET

66 **This icy treat is wicked. We've called it surprise sorbet because people get a big surprise when they discover what's in it, for some reason it doesn't taste like oranges and grapes at all.** **99**

THINK AHEAD WARNING! You need to freeze the fruit for at least 8 hours so it's a good idea to do this the night before you make the sorbet.

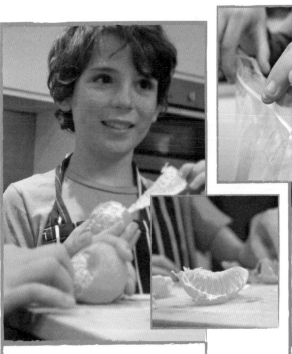

1 Peel the oranges and break them into segments. Make sure there are no stalks left on the grapes.

2 Place the orange segments and grapes in a freezer bag, seal it up and freeze until the fruit is solid.

Make sure that you tightly seal the bag.

3 Once frozen solid, tip the fruit into a food processor or blender.

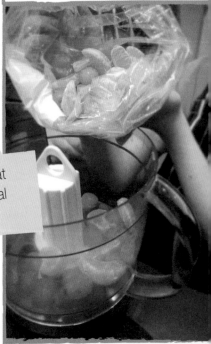

Eek – this is extremely noisy!

4 Add the maple syrup and cinnamon.

5 Ask an adult to help blitz until it has turned to fruity snow.

If you do refreeze it, it's a good idea to blitz it again in a food processor or blender just before serving so that it is lovely and soft.

6 Eat the sorbet straight away or spoon it into a freezer-proof container and put it back into the freezer until you want to eat it.

INSTANT BERRY ICE CREAM

Try this recipe for a super quick and super delicious homemade ice cream. Frozen berries are easy to find in the supermarket at any time of year.

1 Place 400g (14oz) frozen berries in the bowl of a blender or food processor.
2 Add 125g (½ cup) of natural or berry-flavoured yoghurt.
3 Add 3 tablespoons of runny honey.

4 ADULT HELP ALERT Ask an adult to help blitz until it is lovely and creamy. Scrape the sides of the bowl now and then with a spatula.
5 Taste the mixture. Depending on the sharpness of the berries and yoghurt, you might need to add a little more honey.
6 Eat straight away or pour into a freezer-proof container and freeze until you're ready to tuck in.

MAGIC LEMON PUDDING

YOU NEED

* 60g (2oz) softened butter, plus extra for greasing
* 2 large lemons
* 150g (⅔ cup) sugar
* 4 eggs
* 1 heaped teaspoon cornflour (corn starch)
* 30g (2 tablespoons) self-raising (self-rising) flour
* 285ml (1¼ cups) milk

< SERVES 4–6 >

" It goes into the oven as batter and comes out as a cake with delicious lemon sauce underneath. Ta dah! This takes a little bit of work, but it's very impressive. Don't be put off by cooking the pudding in a water bath. It's dead easy. "

TOP TIP Check you have the right size dish by filling a measuring jug with 1 litre (1 quart) of water and pouring this in. If the water almost reaches the top, the dish is the right size.

1 Set the oven to 160°C/325°F/Gas Mark 3. Use a piece of paper towel to wipe some butter around the sides and base of a deep ovenproof dish that holds 1 litre (1 quart) of liquid.

The zest is the top layer of yellow skin – don't grate the white pith below.

2 Finely grate the lemon zest using the method on page 9.

3 Carefully cut the lemons in half using the claw method on page 8 and squeeze out all of the juice.

4 Put the butter, sugar and lemon zest in a mixing bowl and beat with electric beaters (or a wooden spoon if you're strong) until pale and creamy.

64

TOP TIP If your butter is too hard (or you forgot to take it out of the fridge!) grate it into the mixing bowl. This will make it easier to beat with the sugar and lemon zest.

I love doing this bit!

5 Separate the eggs (you can use the fun method on page 9). Put the whites into a very clean mixing bowl and the yolks into the butter mixture.

6 Beat the butter mixture with the egg yolks until it is all well mixed together.

It's not looking so good at the moment, but that's normal!

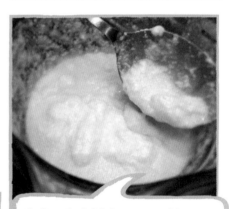

7 Stir the cornflour and flour into the batter. Beat in a splash of milk and a little lemon juice. Keep adding the milk and juice until it is all used up.

8 Whisk the egg whites. Electric beaters are easiest but a whisk works well. Whisk for about 5 minutes or until the egg whites stand up on their own. If you tip the bowl over your head nothing should fall out!

9 Gently fold the egg white into the mixture spoonful by spoonful. Use a large metal spoon or a spatula.

10 Boil some water in a kettle.

ADULT HELP ALERT!

13 It is ready when it is golden on top and coming away from the sides of the tin. Leave to cool in the tin on a wire rack. Leave to settle for 30 minutes. Eat with ice cream!

12 Pour the boiling water into the tray until halfway up the sides of the dish. Wearing gloves, gently slide into the oven. Set the timer for 1 hour.

11 Pour the batter into the baking dish. Carefully place this in a baking tray.

STICKY TOFFEE PUDDING IN A JAR

❝ **These are little jars of pudding heaven! Tell the person who does the shopping that the jars need to hold about 250ml (1 cup) and must be ovenproof. Jam jars or preserving jars are perfect! P.S. If you can't find muscovado sugar, just replace it with soft brown sugar.** ❞

YOU NEED

* 25g (!oz) softened butter, plus extra for greasing
* 100g (3½oz) pitted dates
* ½ teaspoon bicarbonate of soda (baking soda)
* 30g (2 tablespoons) soft brown sugar
* 30g (2 tablespoons) dark muscovado sugar
* 1 egg
* 1 tablespoon golden syrup
* 80g (¾ cup) self-raising (self-rising) flour

FOR THE TOFFEE SAUCE

* 200ml (scant 1 cup) double (heavy) cream
* 50g (¼ cup) soft brown sugar
* 25g (1 oz) butter
* 1½ tablespoons golden syrup

< MAKES 4 >

1 Set the oven to 180°C/350°F/ Gas Mark 4.

2 Butter the insides of the jars using a piece of paper towel. Make sure the sides and bottom are completely covered.

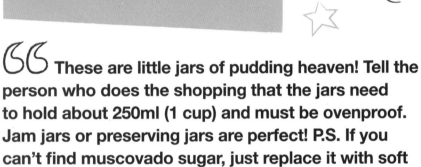

3 Carefully chop the dates into small pieces using the method on page 8 and put them into a bowl.

4 Sprinkle over the bicarbonate of soda and put the kettle on to boil.

5 Very carefully measure out 250ml (1 cup) of boiling water and pour this over the dates. Set the bowl aside.

ADULT HELP ALERT!

6 Put the butter into a mixing bowl. Add both sugars and mix well using electric beaters. It should almost look creamy.

7 Crack in the egg and beat well. Then add the golden syrup and beat again.

8 Add the flour and stir with a wooden spoon until it's just mixed. Pour in the dates and water mixture and stir well.

A ladle works really well.

9 Carefully half-fill the jars with the batter. Try not to get it everywhere – it's quite runny!

10 Wipe any splodges off the jars and place on a baking sheet that has a rim (so they don't slide off). Bake for 20 minutes.

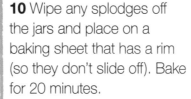

11 While you're waiting, put all the toffee sauce ingredients in a small pan. Set the pan over a medium heat and stir constantly as it comes to the boil.

12 Turn the heat down and let it bubble, stirring now and then, until deliciously smooth and thick.

13 Use oven gloves to take the sponges out of the oven. They should be golden and springy if you lightly touch them on top.

14 Spoon over some of the toffee sauce and pour the rest into a jug. Serve with a scoop of ice cream and the extra sauce on the table. Heaven!

CHOCOLATE PUFFBALLS

66 **These are so much fun! You need a super-strong arm to beat the dough but otherwise it's easy – just look at the spectacular results! P.S. I made 2 lots of these to make my tower but 1 lot will still make an impressive puffball pile.** 99

YOU NEED

* 90g (3oz) butter, plus extra for greasing

* 3 eggs

* 110g (generous 1 cup) plain (all-purpose) flour

* 300ml (1¼ cups) double (heavy) cream, for whipping

* 2 tablespoons icing (confectioners') sugar

FOR THE CHOCOLATE SAUCE

* 100g (3½oz) milk chocolate

* 15g (1 tablespoon) butter

< **MAKES** about 16 >

1 Set the oven to 200°C/400°F/ Gas Mark 6.

2 Use a sheet of paper towel to rub a baking sheet with butter.

3 Crack the eggs into a bowl and whisk with a fork.

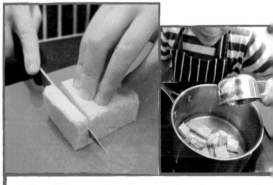

4 Carefully cut the butter into pieces and place in a pan. Pour in 200ml (¾ cup) of cold water. Don't turn the heat on yet – just leave the pan on the hob.

5 Sift the flour and set aside.

6 Set the pan over a medium-high heat. Stir the butter a little to help it melt. As soon as the butter melts and the water boils (big bubbles not little bubbles) turn off the heat.

7 Pour in the flour and start beating. Be careful, as the pan will be hot. You will need good strong arms for this!

8 The mixture will look gloopy to start but keep going until you have a smooth dough that comes away from the sides of the pan in a lump.

9 Start adding the eggs bit by bit. You have to beat hard to mix them in but keep going! You should end up with a thick, smooth and glossy dough.

Leave space around them to puff up.

10 Put tablespoons of the mixture on the baking sheet and place in the oven. Set the timer for 30 minutes.

11 Wear oven gloves to take out of the oven. They should be puffed and golden. Use a skewer to poke a hole to let steam out. Place on a wire rack to cool.

12 Place the cream and icing sugar in a bowl and use an electric whisk to beat until thick.

15 Carefully cut the puffs in half, spoon a dollop of cream on one half and put the top on. Spoon the chocolate sauce on top. Repeat with the rest.

13 To make the chocolate sauce, fill a pan one-quarter full with water and bring to a boil. Meanwhile, break the chocolate into a heatproof bowl and add the butter.

14 When the water boils, turn off the heat. Place the chocolate bowl on top. Stir until it has all melted into a lovely shiny sauce.

Make into a tower or just eat!

MAKE IT UP
CUPCAKES

Use your imagination and add your favourite ingredients to make these cupcakes your own. We've listed a few tasty ideas opposite. As you can see, the recipe is super easy to remember.

YOU NEED

* 220g (8oz) self-raising (self-rising) flour
* 220g (8oz) caster (superfine) sugar
* 220g (8oz) softened butter
* 4 eggs

FOR THE ICING (FROSTING)

* 400g (3 cups) icing (confectioners') sugar
* 100ml (7 tablespoons) lemon juice or milk
* 1 tablespoon cocoa powder (optional)
* Sugar sprinkles (optional)

< **MAKES** about 16 >

1 Set the oven to 180°C/350°F/Gas Mark 4.

2 Place the flour and sugar in a large bowl. Add the butter.

3 Crack in the eggs.

4 Mix well so that all the ingredients are combined and the batter is pale, smooth and fluffy.

5 Now's the time to gently stir in any extra ingredients, if you're using them. Our suggestions are on the opposite page.

6 Line a muffin tin with paper cases. This makes 16 cupcakes, so you will need 2 tins or cook them in 2 batches.

TOP TIP If the cases aren't staying in place, wipe a little butter in the holes of the tray and press down the cases so that they stick.

7 Spoon the batter into the cases until three-quarters full.

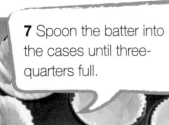

8 Place in the oven (*ah! gloves!*) Set the timer for 18 minutes.

Time to lick your fingers and tidy up!

Stick a toothpick into one and if it comes out clean, they're ready. If there is batter stuck to the toothpick cook them for another 2 minutes.

10 Leave to cool in the tray for a bit and then lift them onto a wire rack. When they're completely cold you can ice them if you like.

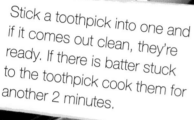

9 When the timer goes off check the cupcakes. They should have risen and be lightly golden.

TOP TIP Spread the icing out with a wet finger to make it really smooth.

11 To make the icing, mix the icing sugar and lemon juice or milk together in a bowl. Add the cocoa powder if you want chocolate icing.

12 Spoon icing onto each cake. Add sprinkles if you like.

VARIATIONS

Try adding one of these extra ingredients to the batter.

SULTANA CUPCAKES
Add 125g (4½oz) sultanas.

BERRY CUPCAKES
Add 200g (7oz) fresh blueberries or 200g (7oz) chopped raspberries or blackberries.

CHOCOLATE CUPCAKES
Add 4 tablespoons of cocoa powder.

VANILLA CUPCAKES
Add 2 teaspoons vanilla extract.

SERIOUSLY GOOD

CHOCOLATE

BROWNIES

Yum. That's all there is to say about these. Sometimes brownies are a bit too rich but we think these are just right. If you want to experiment, try adding a small handful of dried fruit or nuts to the mix instead of the chocolate buttons.

1 Set the oven to 180°C/350°F/ Gas Mark 4.

2 Line a 20cm (8in) square baking tin with foil.

3 Fill a pan one-quarter full with water, set over a high heat and bring to the boil.

4 While you're waiting for this to happen, break the dark chocolate into very small pieces and cut up the butter.

5 Place the dark chocolate and butter in a heatproof bowl big enough to sit comfortably on top of your pan of water. A metal bowl is perfect.

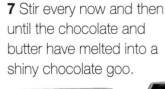

7 Stir every now and then until the chocolate and butter have melted into a shiny chocolate goo.

6 When the water has come to the boil, very carefully take it off the heat and sit the bowl with the chocolate and butter in it on top.

8 While this is happening, crack the eggs into a separate bowl, add the sugar and vanilla and beat until creamy.

11 Stir in the chocolate buttons. Tip into the baking tin.

9 Carefully pour the melted chocolate mixture into the egg mixture and beat some more.

10 Sift in the flour and beat again.

WARNING
It will be hot!

14 These are lovely served warm with vanilla ice cream and sprinkles. Of course, they're also great cold!

Wear oven gloves or ask an adult to help.

12 Place the tin on a baking sheet and place it in the oven. Set the timer for 25 minutes.

13 Once firm on top but soft to the touch, take it out of the oven. Leave to cool slightly in the tin and then lift out using the foil. Cut into squares.

CHRISTMAS DECORATION BISCUITS

YOU NEED

* 400g (4 cups) plain (all-purpose) flour
* A pinch of salt
* 2 teaspoons ground cinnamon
* 2 teaspoons ground ginger
* 2 teaspoons allspice
* 200g (7oz) soft butter
* 150g (1 cup) icing (confectioners') sugar
* 1 teaspoon vanilla extract
* 1 egg

FOR THE ICING (FROSTING)

* 400g (3 cups) icing (confectioners') sugar
* 100ml (7 tablespoons) lemon juice or milk
* Natural food colouring
* Sugar sprinkles and decorations

< **MAKES** about 40 (depending on how big you cut them) >

66 **We make these every Christmas and they look really cool on the Christmas tree. But you can make them for any celebration in any shape you like. Hearts for Valentine's Day and ghosts for Halloween are really good.** 99

Cinnamon smells delish!

You can do this by hand with a wooden spoon but you'll need to work hard.

This might make a bit of a mess as the sugar flies out!

1 Mix the flour, salt, cinnamon, ginger and allspice in a bowl. Put the bowl aside – you'll come back to it later.

2 Put the butter, sugar and vanilla in another bowl and beat with electric beaters until pale and creamy.

3 Crack in the egg and beat.

The mixture might look a bit weird and curdled but that's fine.

It will look a bit like rubble.

4 Tip in the flour mixture, then beat on a low speed until combined. Scrape down the sides of the bowl a couple of times to make sure all the flour is mixed in.

I like to use the karate chop method!

5 This is the fun bit. Bring the mixture together with your hands to make a lump of dough.

7 Shape each piece into an oval, wrap in greaseproof paper and chill in the fridge for 30 minutes.

6 Tip it onto your work top and divide it into 2 equal pieces.

Plenty of time for cleaning up!

Don't forget to keep turning the dough or it will stick.

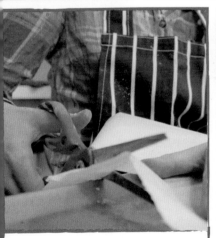

8 Take the dough out of the fridge and set your oven to 170°C/325°F/Gas Mark 3. Line a baking sheet with baking paper.

9 Sprinkle your work surface with a little flour. Place a piece of dough on top. Start with your rolling pin in the middle of the dough and gently push it away from you. Bring the rolling pin back to the middle and then roll it towards you. Turn the dough a bit and roll again. Continue like this until the dough is about 3mm (0.1in) thick.

11 Lift the shapes onto the baking sheet with a fish slice.

12 Put the baking sheet in the oven. Set the timer for 8 minutes. Don't wander off! Keep a close eye on the biscuits as they burn easily. They should be a pale gold when they're cooked, so take them out earlier if they're looking too dark.

10 Cut out your shapes using biscuit cutters or a glass.

13 Using oven gloves, take the tray out of the oven.

Repeat with the rest of the dough.

14 Using a skewer, make a hole in the top of each shape as soon as they come out of the oven. Don't make the hole too close to the edge. Wiggle it to make the hole big enough for a ribbon.

15 Leave the biscuits on the baking sheet for a few minutes and then slide them onto a wire rack to cool and crisp up.

We like to add lemon juice so the icing's not too sweet.

16 While the biscuits are cooling, put the icing sugar into a bowl. Add the milk or lemon juice and stir until glossy and smooth.

17 Spoon the icing into little bowls – one for each different colour icing you want to make. Add a different food colouring to each bowl.

18 When the biscuits are completely cool, start decorating. You can use a teaspoon or a small blunt knife, but actually wet fingers work best. Add the decorations and sprinkles, gently pressing them in.

So pretty!

19 Let the icing dry completely before you thread the biscuits with ribbon and hang them on the tree.

6

OUT AND ABOUT

STICKY CHICKEN DRUMSTICKS

YOU NEED

* 4 tablespoons tomato ketchup
* 4 tablespoons soy sauce
* 1 tablespoon olive oil
* 2 tablespoons honey
* 2 garlic cloves
* 1 lemon
* 1 teaspoon Chinese five spice
* 1 teaspoon French mustard
* 10 chicken drumsticks

< **MAKES** 10 drumsticks >

" **These are so easy to make and really cool to take with you when you're on the move. Make the potato salad (pages 82–83) to go with them if you want a real feast.** "

Action Man will help with this one!

1 First, make the marinade. Put the ketchup, soy sauce, olive oil and honey in a jug.

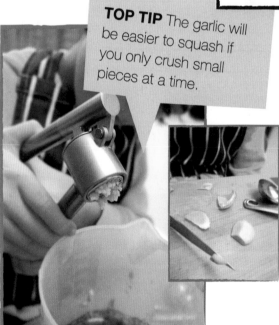

TOP TIP The garlic will be easier to squash if you only crush small pieces at a time.

2 Peel the garlic cloves and cut them in half if they're big. Place in a garlic press and squeeze the handles. This can be tough! Scrape into the jug.

3 Cut the lemon in half using the claw method on page 8. Squeeze out the juice using a lemon squeezer. Pour the juice into the jug.

TOP TIP Press the lemon down on the squeezer and twist at the same time.

It does smell quite strong at this point, but don't worry, it will just make the chicken tender, juicy and full of flavour.

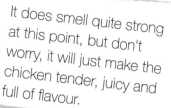

5 Put the drumsticks into a shallow bowl or tray – anything that will fit them snugly.

Yep, it does feel rather squishy, but it's worth it!

4 Stir in the Chinese five spice and mustard.

6 Pour over the marinade and massage it into the chicken really well.

This is a good time to tidy up – or play!

ADULT HELP ALERT!

8 Just before you cook them, set the oven to 200°C/ 400°F/Gas Mark 6.

9 Lift the drumsticks out of the marinade and put them in a baking tray. Set the spare marinade aside – you'll need it later.

7 Leave the drumsticks for 30 minutes (or longer) to soak up the flavours.

10 Using oven gloves, put the baking tray in the oven. Set the timer for 15 minutes.

11 When it goes off, use oven gloves to very carefully take the tray out of the oven.

13 Return to the oven for 15 minutes. When cooked they will be golden, sticky and the meat should be white.

These smell so wonderful dogs will probably follow you!

12 While in the tray, brush with some marinade, then use tongs to turn them over. Brush with more marinade.

Enjoy them hot or cold.

DADDY'S BRILLIANT POTATO SALAD

* 2 eggs
* 600g (1lb 5oz) new potatoes
* 2 slices of smoked ham
* 3 spring onions (scallions)
* A knob of butter
* 2 dessertspoons mayonnaise

< SERVES 4–6 >

66 **Our dad taught us how to make this – he's a great cook! This is a fantastic dish to take on a picnic. No matter how much you make, there never seems to be enough!** 99

3 Now start chopping! Cut each potato in half and in half again using the method on page 8. Place the pieces in a saucepan.

You want big bubbles not fizzy drink bubbles.

1 Put the eggs in a pan and cover with cold water.

2 Set the pan over a high heat. As soon as the water starts to boil, turn off the heat and cover with a lid. Set the timer for 7 minutes.

We keep the skin on the potatoes!

4 Cut the ham into strips, then into smaller pieces.

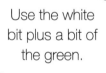

Use the white bit plus a bit of the green.

5 Cut the hairy end off the spring onion and slice into very thin rings. Set aside.

6 When the timer goes off, tip out the hot water and run the eggs under cold water to stop them cooking. Set aside.

7 Just cover the potatoes with cold water and set the pan over a high heat.

If it looks like it's going to boil over, turn down the heat a little.

ADULT HELP ALERT!

8 When the water boils, turn the heat down to medium. Cook for 10 minutes.

9 Peel the eggs and chop into bite-size pieces.

10 When cooked, very carefully drain the potatoes into a colander, give them a shake and then tip them back into the pan.

ADULT HELP ALERT!

TOP TIP
Add the butter when the potatoes are still warm so they absorb the buttery flavour.

13 Very gently stir until everything is covered in mayonnaise.

Eat hot or cold!

11 Add the butter and stir to coat all of the potatoes.

12 Add the ham, onions, eggs and mayonnaise.

CHICKEN FAJITAS

66 **This is one of our favourite recipes. It's really tasty but the best bit is assembling it and adding the stuff you like. Plus, it's portable so you can take it with you when you're busy!** 99

YOU NEED

* 2 chicken breasts
* 2 teaspoons smoked paprika
* ½ teaspoon ground cumin
* 1 teaspoon dried oregano
* A pinch of cayenne pepper or chilli powder
* 1 lime
* 2 tablespoons olive oil
* 1 red (bell) pepper
* 1 onion
* 4 flour tortillas or wraps

< SERVES 4 >

Eww! The chicken feels gooey like slugs!

Now go and wash your hands, chopping boards and knives.

1 Carefully cut the chicken into long thin strips following the cutting method on page 8. Place in a bowl.

THINGS YOU MIGHT WANT TO ADD

Guacamole (pages 110–111)
Natural yoghurt
Sour cream
Grated cheese
Shredded lettuce
Chopped tomato
Mixed beans
Cooked rice

3 Cut the lime in half and use a lemon squeezer to get out all the juice. Pour into the bowl with the chicken and spices.

If you like it spicy add ¼ of a teaspoon of cayenne or chilli powder.

2 Add the paprika, cumin, oregano and cayenne pepper or chilli powder.

4 Add 1 tablespoon of the olive oil.

Now it looks like red slugs!

5 Using a big spoon, stir everything together. Set the bowl aside.

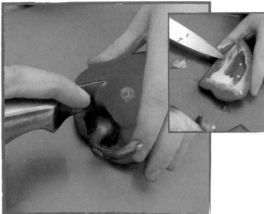

6 Carefully cut the pepper in half using the method on page 8. Cut each piece in half again and remove the white bits and seeds.

7 Thinly slice each piece of pepper. Be watchful of those fingers! Place in a bowl.

You want sliced onion here, not chopped onion!

8 Slice the onion into half-moon shapes following the method on page 8. Add to the pepper bowl.

10 Check whether the oil is hot by putting a piece of pepper in the pan – if it makes a loud sizzle it's ready.

ADULT HELP ALERT!

9 Set a large griddle pan or frying pan over a high heat and add the final tablespoon of oil.

11 Using tongs put the chicken, onion and pepper into the pan and mix together.

12 Set your timer for 5 minutes. Turn everything over quite a lot with your tongs during this time.

13 To check if the chicken is ready, cut a piece in half. If it's pink in the middle it needs to cook a bit more, but if it's white inside and golden on the outside it's done! When cooked, take off the heat.

Don't pile on too much or your fajita won't roll up!

14 Put some chicken in the middle of your tortilla or wrap and add the other things you like. Fold in the sides and roll up. If you're heading out, wrap in foil and off you go!

CONFETTI ENERGY BALLS

We were going to call this edible playdough as it's fun to make it into wacky shapes! These little bites taste fantastic and are great to have in the backpack to snack on when you're out and about with mates.

Dried apricots are my favourite healthy food!

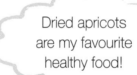

1 Tip the oats into a food processor or blender. Make sure the lid is on tight and then whizz until the oats look like powder.

ADULT HELP ALERT!

2 Add everything else (except the sprinkles).

3 Whizz until the mixture comes together into a lump. This will take longer than you think, but be patient and keep going – it will happen after a minute or so!

Eeek!
It is so noisy!

4 Tip the lump into a large bowl. Now for the good bit – adding the sprinkles! A spoon doesn't really work so you need to use your hands to mix the sprinkles in evenly.

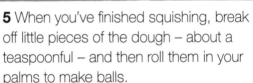

5 When you've finished squishing, break off little pieces of the dough – about a teaspoonful – and then roll them in your palms to make balls.

6 Or make funny shapes if you want to!

8 These travel really well in a plastic container so pack them into your backpack when you're going out with your mates.

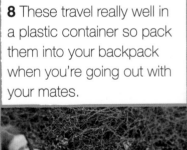

7 You can eat these straight away, or put them in the fridge for an hour or so first to let them firm up a bit.

POSH NOSH

AWESOME STICKY RIBS

" Juicy, sticky and oh so tasty, these ribs are the best. You don't need knives or forks – just tuck in with your fingers. Daddy's Brilliant Potato Salad on pages 82–83 is delicious with them. "

It smells like a witch's brew!

1 Mix everything except the ribs together in a bowl to make a marinade.

2 Whisk well to dissolve all of the sugar.

3 Put the ribs in a large shallow bowl and pour over half the marinade. Set the rest aside for later.

4 Get mucky and rub the marinade into the ribs with your hands! They all need to be completely covered.

5 Cover with cling film (plastic wrap) and marinate in the fridge. The ribs will be brilliant if you leave them to soak up all the flavours for 2 hours, but less is fine if you don't have the time.

SAFETY TIPS
Always wash your hands immediately after touching raw meat and always marinate meat in the refrigerator.

6 Just before you take the ribs out of the fridge set the oven to 150°C/300°F/Gas Mark 2.

Cover tightly with tin foil – make sure it's sealed well.

7 Put the ribs into a large baking tray that's large enough to hold them in a single layer.

ADULT HELP ALERT!

9 When the timer goes off use oven gloves to carefully take the tray out of the oven. Remove the tin foil and brush the ribs with some of the marinade you set aside. Turn the oven up to its hottest setting.

8 Wearing oven gloves, slide the tray into the oven. Set the timer for 1½ hours.

10 Using oven gloves, put the ribs back in the oven without the foil and set the timer for 25 minutes.

SUNSHINE ALERT: If it's sunny, cook the ribs on a very hot barbecue grill instead of in the oven for the last 25 minutes. Cook for about 10 minutes, turning regularly so that they don't burn.

The kitchen will soon start to smell amazing as the ribs get lovely and sticky.

11 Serve the ribs with some of the spare marinade poured over. And a napkin to wipe your hands!

DREAMY CHICKEN CURRY

" You can make this delicious creamy curry as spicy as you like. If you don't want it spicy at all, leave out the cayenne pepper. If you want it a bit fiery, add 1 full teaspoon. You don't have to add fish sauce but it will add bags of flavour. "

YOU NEED

* 1 onion
* 4 garlic cloves
* 50g (1¾oz) trimmed green beans
* 6 skinless chicken breasts
* 2 tablespoons vegetable oil
* 1 teaspoon turmeric
* ½ teaspoon ground ginger
* 1 teaspoon mild curry powder
* ½ teaspoon cayenne pepper (optional)
* 2 x 400ml (14oz) tins (cans) coconut milk
* 2 tablespoons fish sauce (optional)
* 1 lime
* Naan, to serve

< SERVES 4–6 >

1 Finely chop the onion by following the instructions on page 8. Set aside.

3 Cut the beans in half.

2 Peel the garlic and crush the cloves into a small bowl using a garlic press.

ALERT Make sure you wash your hands, the chopping board and the knife really well after cutting up raw chicken.

4 Place the chicken breasts on to a chopping board and, using the method on page 8, slice in half lengthways, then into chunks. Set aside.

Heat 1 tablespoon of the oil in a heavy pan over a medium heat. Add the chicken and fry for 5 minutes, stirring every now and then, until the chicken starts to turn golden.

6 Lift the chicken onto a plate using a large spoon and set aside.

7 Turn the heat down to medium-low and add the other tablespoon of oil and then the onion. Cook for 5 minutes, stirring quite a lot, or until the onion is very soft.

Oops! Broken spice bottle: call an adult if this kind of accident happens!

8 Take the pan off the heat and add the garlic, turmeric, ginger, curry powder and cayenne pepper (if you like). Set over a medium heat, stir and fry for 1 minute.

TOP TIP Before you juice them, roll lemons and limes gently on a work surface, pressing them down as you go. This will help release a lot more juice.

Fish sauce is a bit whiffy, but it will make the curry really tasty.

9 Pour in the coconut milk and fish sauce (if using).

10 Add the chicken and beans and stir. Turn the heat down to medium-low and simmer for 7 minutes.

11 While the curry is cooking, cut the lime in half and squeeze out the juice. When the curry is cooked, pour this in.

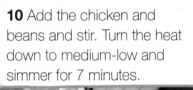

You just want a few bubbles – if you let the curry boil, the chicken will be tough.

12 Serve the curry with delicious naan bread. Yum.

LEMON AND
GARLIC PRAWN
SKEWERS

" Even if you think you don't like prawns, we bet you like these because they're super sweet and tasty! You can cook them on a barbecue but if you do, soak the skewers in water for 30 minutes first so they don't catch fire! "

1 If your prawns still have skin and heads on, peel these off following the instructions in the blue box.

HOW TO PEEL PRAWNS
Grip the prawn just underneath the head and then twist the head off and throw it away. Peel the legs and shell off starting at the bottom of the prawn near the head. You might be able to get it off in one go!

2 Using the method on page 8, cut one of the lemons in half and squeeze out the juice. Cut the other lemon in half lengthways and in half again.

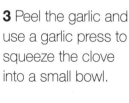

3 Peel the garlic and use a garlic press to squeeze the clove into a small bowl.

4 Add the chilli flakes, lemon juice, oil and fish sauce (if you're using it). Stir with a fork.

Pour this mixture over the prawns and mix well, with your hands if you like.

This is good gooey fun!

6 Cover with cling film (plastic wrap) and marinate in the fridge for 30 minutes. Now's the time to soak your skewers if you're barbecuing!

7 Carefully thread both sides of 3 prawns onto a skewer. Try to skewer them through the top and the bottom.

8 Set a griddle or frying pan over a high heat and wait until it's really hot (if you're barbecuing make sure the grill is very hot as well).

9 Place the skewers on the pan and set the timer for 2 minutes. The prawns will turn pink, like magic.

10 Using tongs, turn the skewers over and cook for a further 2 minutes.

11 The prawns are done when they are gorgeously golden and charred in parts. Serve with the lemon wedges and a sprinkle of salt.

ROAST CHICKEN

AND VEGETABLES

❝ **This is a fantastic way to cook a wonderful meal for the whole family. Even some adults find it tricky to get the timing right for a roast dinner, but it's not hard if you do it this way. The results are really impressive!** ❞

YOU NEED

* 50g (2oz) butter
* 1 lemon
* 2 garlic cloves
* 1 medium chicken (about 1.3kg/3lb)
* 4 medium carrots
* 12 new potatoes
* 1 tablespoon olive oil
* Salt and pepper
* 200g (1⅓ cups) frozen peas

< SERVES 4 >

1 Set the oven to 230°C/450°F/Gas Mark 8.

2 Chop the butter into pieces. Cut the lemon in half using the method on page 8.

3 Peel the garlic, cutting off the tough ends if you need to.

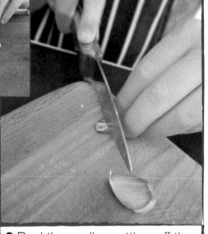

4 Place the chicken in the largest baking tray that you can find.

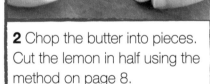

5 Snip off any string that's tied around the bird. Open up the legs so that the heat can circulate inside.

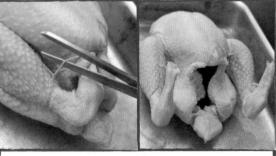

6 Use your hands to smear butter all over the chicken.

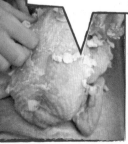

7 Squeeze over the lemon juice (pick out any seeds) and put the halves inside the cavity.

You could place some fresh herbs in the cavity — use thyme, parsley or tarragon.

8 Stuff the garlic inside the cavity.

9 Put the carrots and potatoes into a large bowl and pour over the oil. Mix with your hands so that the veg is coated.

Sprinkle over some salt and pepper.

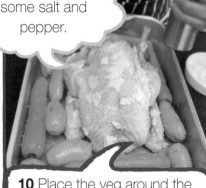

10 Place the veg around the chicken. Try to keep it in one layer but if the tray is not large enough, tuck some underneath the chicken.

11 Wear oven gloves to place in the oven. Turn down to 190°C/375°F/Gas Mark 5. Set the timer for 1 hour.

12 To check if the chicken is ready, pull a leg away and stick a skewer where the leg joins the body. Some juice will run out: if it's yellowy/clear, the chicken is ready. If pink, the chicken needs to cook for a little longer.

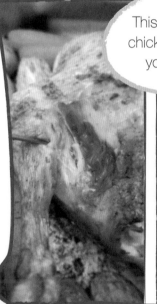

This will keep the chicken warm until you're ready.

13 Place back in the oven. Switch the oven off and leave the door ajar.

14 Half fill a pan with water, set over a high heat and bring to the boil. Carefully add the peas and cook for about 5 minutes.

15 Carefully drain the peas in a colander and tip into a serving bowl.

16 Using oven gloves, remove the chicken from the oven and place on a board. Tip the pan juices into a gravy jug.

ADULT HELP ALERT!

RASPBERRY

RAINBOW SALAD

" This bright salad is lovely and you can add whatever veggies or fruit you like. Try to get in lots of different colours and at least one fruit. The dressing is slightly sweet and really yummy. "

YOU NEED

FOR THE SALAD DRESSING

* 90ml (⅓ cup) vegetable oil
* ½ teaspoon Dijon mustard
* 2 tablespoons raspberry vinegar
* A squeeze of lime juice
* A pinch of salt and a grind of pepper

FOR THE SALAD

* 1 medium courgette (zucchini), washed well
* 1 small carrot, washed well
* 2 large lettuce leaves
* 8 cherry tomatoes
* ½ red (bell) pepper
* A small handful of blueberries
* 4 tablespoons sweetcorn

< SERVES 4 as a side salad **>**

It's made little raspberry bubbles...

1 Put the dressing ingredients in a jar. Shake!

2 Using a vegetable peeler, carefully cut the courgette and carrot into ribbons using the method on page 9. Press down gently to get nice big, long strips. The skin is fine to eat!

3 Stop peeling the courgette when you get to the seedy part in the centre. Place in a salad bowl.

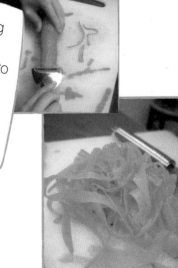

98

4 Roll up the lettuce leaves and finely slice. Add to the bowl.

5 Using the method on page 8, halve the tomatoes. Cut the pepper into strips and then into small pieces. Add to the bowl.

> I could eat a whole can of sweetcorn!

6 Mix the blueberries and sweetcorn and add to the bowl filled with the salad.

> This tastes as good as it looks. Promise!

7 Add 2 tablespoons of dressing to the salad and use tongs to mix it all together.

OTHER TASTY SALADS

CRUNCHY CARROT

1 Carefully peel and grate 4 large carrots.
2 Place the carrots in a medium-sized bowl. Add a few tablespoons of sultanas and a small handful of chopped parsley.
3 Add 2 tablespoons of flaked almonds if you like – it makes the salad extra crunchy.
4 Make the salad dressing as for the Raspberry Rainbow Salad and pour 2 tablespoons over the carrot mixture.
5 Toss with tongs or clean hands.

APPLE, CELERY AND CUCUMBER

1 Take 1 medium-sized cucumber and make ribbons with a peeler following the instructions on the left.
2 Take 2 celery sticks and carefully slice them into chunks.
3 Carefully cut 1 apple in half and then cut each half in half. Cut out and discard the seedy bits and core from each apple quarter. Chop into small pieces.
4 Make the salad dressing for the Raspberry Rainbow Salad and pour 2 tablespoons over the apple, celery and cucumber mixture.
5 Toss with tongs or clean hands.

FANCY LAMB

⭐ ⭐ ⭐

YOU NEED

* 1 lamb neck fillet
* Olive oil, for brushing
* Sea salt flakes
* Freshly ground black pepper
* 1 teaspoon dried rosemary (optional)
* 1 egg
* 1 sheet ready-rolled puff pastry

< SERVES 2 >

If you want to cook a fancy dinner for the adults in your house then this will really impress them. The lamb wrapped up in its pastry blanket looks really professional – just don't tell them how easy it is to make!

1 Set the oven to 200°C/ 400°F/Gas Mark 7. Line a baking sheet with baking paper.

2 Place the lamb on a chopping board and carefully cut in half.

3 Brush the fillets all over with a little bit of oil.

Rosemary adds lots of flavour.

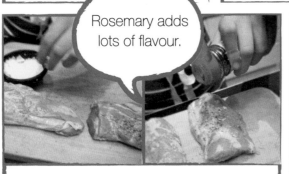

4 Sprinkle with salt, pepper and the rosemary (if you're using it).

5 Set a frying pan over a high heat for a couple of minutes. Carefully place your hand above it to check if it's hot enough – you should feel the heat.

6 Using tongs, gently place the fillets in the pan.

BEWARE: It may get a little smoky!

7 Cook for about 1 minute then carefully turn the fillets over using tongs.

8 Keep turning every minute until the fillets are lovely and brown all over – even the ends! Take the fillets out of the pan and let cool a little.

9 Crack the egg into a small bowl and whisk with a fork.

10 Place the pastry sheet on a clean chopping board. Place one of the lamb fillets along the edge closest to you.

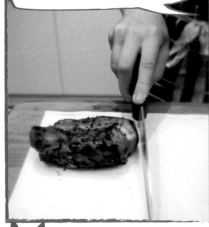

11 Using a knife, cut the pastry in half so that the lamb fits.

12 Tightly roll the pastry around the lamb. Brush the end of the pastry with egg to "glue" the parcel closed. Pinch the sides together to close. Place on the baking sheet. Roll up the other fillet in the same way.

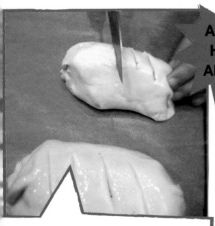

ADULT HELP ALERT!

13 Very carefully make cuts in the top of the parcels. This will allow steam to escape. Brush with egg.

14 Wearing oven gloves, slide the baking sheet into the oven and set the timer for 20 minutes. When they're done, the pastry parcels should be puffed and golden.

Enjoy with some delicious crunchy vegetables!

FLOWERPOT BREAD
OR PIZZA DOUGH

GOING
POTTY

66 **This is such a cool recipe. It makes two impressive flowerpots of bread, or four big pizza bases. If you're making pizza, follow steps 4–9 and then go to pages 46–47 for the pizza recipe.** 99

66 **Use pots about 10cm (4in) wide and 10cm (4in) high. You need to fill them almost to the top with dough. The pots must be made of terracotta and be absolutely clean. New is best.** 99

YOU NEED

* 80g (2¾oz) butter, plus a bit more for greasing

* 450g (4½ cups) self-raising (self-rising) flour, plus about 1 teaspoon more for flouring the pots

* 1 teaspoon salt

* 250–300ml (generous 1 cup–1¼ cups) milk, plus extra for brushing

< **MAKES** 2 flowerpot loaves >

1 Set the oven to 200°C/400°F/ Gas Mark 6.

2 First, prepare the flowerpots. Grease the insides with butter. Use a bit of paper towel to spread it round.

The pot has to be really well covered or the bread might get stuck.

3 Hold the pot sideways and sprinkle in about ½ teaspoon of flour. Turn the pot, shaking it as you go, until the insides are covered in flour.

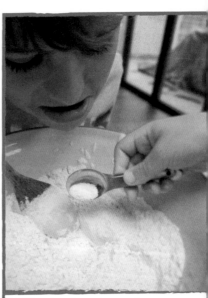

4 Tip the flour into a large bowl and add the salt. Stir.

It feels amazingly soft!

5 Cut up and add the butter. Rub it into the flour with your fingers. You don't want any lumps of butter left.

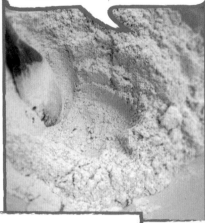

6 Make a hole in the flour so that you can see the bottom of the bowl. This is called a "well".

EPIC FAIL ALERT
Gradually add in just enough milk to make a sticky dough.

7 Stir in the milk and the flour bit by bit.

8 When the dough begins to look a bit scraggily, start using your hands.

9 Add a tiny bit more milk to the mixture if the dough is too dry. Shape into a large ball.

10 Carefully cut the dough in half and shape each half into a ball. Put a ball of dough into each flowerpot and brush the top with milk.

11 Wearing oven gloves, put the pots into the oven and set the timer for about 30 minutes. The exact time will depend on the size of your flowerpots so keep an eye on their progress. When it's ready the kitchen should smell like bread and the tops of the loaves should be hard and golden.

12 Leave them to sit in their pots for at least 10 minutes. When the pots are cool enough to handle, very carefully run a flat, blunt knife around the sides between the bread and the pot. Tip upside down. Ta dah!

13 This is best with butter and some honey or jam (jelly). It doesn't stay fresh for long but it tastes brilliant toasted.

8

PARTY TIME

SADIE'S SUPER
SANDWICHES

" Sandwiches can be dull but these are fun to make for parties. Ask the person who does the shopping to see if they can buy high-fibre white bread. Use any filling you like. "

PINWHEELS

TOP TIP
Ask an adult if they want the crusts to make breadcrumbs.

1 Carefully cut the crusts off a slice of bread.

2 Roll the bread flat with a rolling pin.

3 Lightly spread with cream cheese.

5 Sprinkle over the bread and lightly press into the cream cheese.

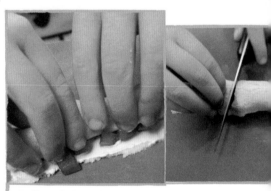

6 Carefully roll up the bread – make sure it's quite tight. Cut the roll into 2cm (¾in) pieces and turn them on their ends so you can see the spiral. Yum.

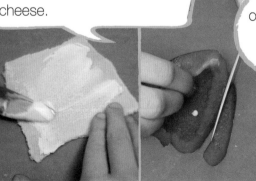

4 Slice a couple of strips off the pepper and cut into very small pieces.

JAMWICHES

1 Take 2 slices of bread and spread one side with butter, and then with jam. Put the other slice on top.

2 Using a cookie cutter press down on the bread. Make sure it cuts all the way through.

Cut out as many shapes as you can, then eat!

FAIRY BREAD

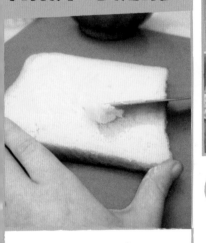

1 Butter a piece of bread right up to the edges.

2 Place on a large plate and scatter sprinkles on top.

3 Shake off any that are loose and cut into pieces.

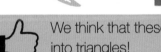

👍 We think that these sandwiches definitely taste best when they are cut into triangles!

STRAWBERRY SANDWICHES

Try this wonderful, summery recipe when you are having an outdoor party or a picnic in the sunshine.

1 Spread 2 pieces of sliced white bread with cream cheese.
2 Remove the green tops from 6 strawberries and thinly slice 4 of the strawberries.
3 Place the sliced strawberries on one of the slices of bread until completely covered and top with the second slice of bread.
4 Cut the sandwich into triangles.
5 Place one triangle on top of another and top with a whole strawberry. Use a toothpick to hold it all together, skewering through the strawberry and all of the sandwich layers.

SAUSAGE ROLLS

YOU NEED

* Vegetable oil, for brushing
* 1 egg
* A few sprigs of fresh parsley
* ½ onion
* 2 garlic cloves
* 100g (3½oz) bacon
* 400g (14oz) minced (ground) pork
* 20g (¾oz) butter
* ½ teaspoon dried thyme
* 1 sheet of ready-rolled puff pastry 36 x 24cm (14 x 9in)

< MAKES 12 >

" Our friends demolish these at parties – if the adults don't get to them first! You can squeeze the meat out of good quality sausages instead of making your own mixture, but we think it's loads better to make these from scratch. "

1 Set the oven to 220°C/ 425°F/ Gas Mark 7.

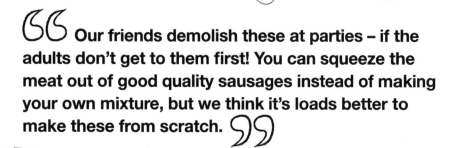

2 Brush a baking sheet with a little bit of oil (or cut out a piece of baking paper and use it to line the baking sheet).

3 Crack the egg into a small bowl and beat lightly with a fork.

4 Roughly chop the parsley and place in the bowl of a food processor.

The garlic is a bit stinky when it's raw but tastes lovely once cooked.

6 Cut the bacon into pieces and add this to the bowl.

The thyme smells gorgeous...

5 Peel the onion and cut it in half using the method on page 8. Peel the garlic. Add both to the processor bowl.

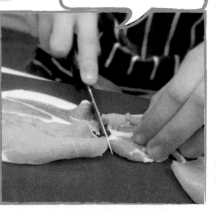

7 Finally, add the pork, butter and thyme.

8 Secure the lid and blitz until the mixture is almost smooth and formed into a ball.

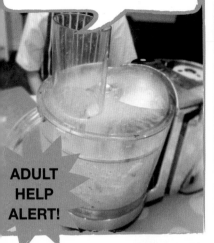

ADULT HELP ALERT!

I don't want any big chunks of onion. Ugh!

9 Carefully tip out the mixture and divide into 2 equal pieces.

10 Lay your pastry on a chopping board and cut it in half lengthways.

HOW TO CUT YOUR PASTRY EQUALLY INTO TWO

Gently fold the pastry over so the bottom edge touches the top edge and press lightly on the fold. When you unfold you will have a line to cut along.

11 Form each half of the mixture into a sausage shape along the length of a piece of pastry. Try to make it neat!

12 Brush the edge of the pastry with egg and then firmly roll it up.

13 Cut the sausage into 6 equal pieces and place them on the baking sheet. Repeat with the remaining pastry and pork mixture.

14 Brush the tops with egg and carefully make a couple of cuts in the top to let the steam out.

15 Wear gloves to place in the oven. Set the timer for 20 minutes. Once done, they will be golden and bubbling and the kitchen should smell wonderful!

GUACAMOLE

" **This tastes so good you wouldn't think it was good for you! It's ideal for parties as everyone can dunk in different vegetables, breadsticks or crisps (chips).** **"**

1 Finely dice the tomato by following the claw method on page 8.

2 Peel the outside papery skin off the spring onion.

3 Cut the hairy bits off the end.

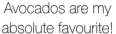

Avocados are my absolute favourite!

4 Very finely slice the spring onion and add to a large bowl with the tomatoes.

5 Cut off the end of the garlic clove, remove the skin and squeeze it into the bowl using a garlic press.

6 Cut the avocado in half around both sides, so that you have cut all the way around.

7 Gently twist both sides until they come apart.

Wahoo! I almost got the whole thing out in one piece!

8 Scoop out the stone with a teaspoon and scoop the flesh into another bowl. Repeat with the other avocado.

I like it really smooth.

9 Mash with a fork. Leave some chunky bits if you like.

10 Tip into the bowl with the tomato mixture. Gently mix everything together.

11 Cut the lime in half using the method on page 8. Squeeze out the juice and pour a little into the avocado mixture.

12 Add a pinch of salt and grind in some black pepper.

13 Add a drop or two of chilli sauce (don't add any more yet!) and stir.

14 Taste! Add more lime juice or chilli sauce if you think it needs it.

CHOCOLATE MERINGUE KISSES

" Making meringues is great fun. If you don't have a piping bag just fill a zip-lock freezer bag with the beaten egg whites and snip a tiny bit off one corner. Instant piping bag! "

YOU NEED

FOR THE MERINGUES
* 3 eggs
* 90g (generous ⅓ cup) caster (superfine) sugar
* ¼ teaspoon cream of tartar
* A few drops of food colouring (optional)

FOR THE CHOCOLATE ICING (FROSTING)
* 100g (3½oz) milk chocolate
* 100ml (7 tablespoons) double (heavy) cream

< **MAKES** 16 kisses >

1 Set the oven to 150°C/300°F/ Gas Mark 3.

2 Cut out 2 rectangles of baking paper and line 2 baking sheets.

3 Separate the eggs using the fun method on page 9.

4 Pour the egg whites into a very clean mixing bowl. Beat with electric beaters until little peaks form. If you can lift the bowl over your head and nothing falls out – it's ready!

5 Sprinkle in the sugar 1 spoonful at a time, beating well after each addition. This makes the mixture go shiny and creamy!

6 Add the cream of tartar and food colouring (if you're using it) and beat for 1 minute more.

Yay! It's gloopy and messy!

7 Fit your piping bag with a star-shaped nozzle. Roll down the top of the bag and half-fill with the egg white.

8 Unfold the bag and gather the top in one hand. With your other hand gently squeeze the mixture down to the nozzle end to get rid of any air bubbles.

9 Hold the bag straight down and squeeze out a little blob onto the baking sheet. Stop squeezing when you've made a 2cm ¾in) blob and lift the bag up quickly to make a little peak. Repeat with the rest of the mixture.

Don't worry if the blobs aren't exactly the same size – they'll still taste great.

10 Wear gloves to slide the baking sheets in the oven. Set the timer for 40–45 minutes. They will be crisp on the outside when they're ready.

11 Switch off the oven, leave the oven door open a bit and leave them to cool.

12 Make the chocolate icing following steps 9–11 on page 115 or just use chocolate spread.

I've made a meringue and chocolate burger!

13 Spread a little chocolate icing on the bottom of a meringue and glue another one to it. Repeat.

AWESOME CHOCOLATE CAKE

66 **This is totally delicious and you can be as artistic as you like with the decorations. You need two round 20cm (8in) cake tins for this recipe – it won't work well if you use a different size.** 99

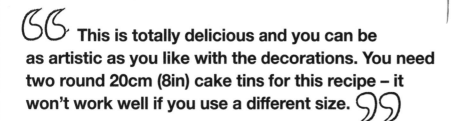

YOU NEED

FOR THE CAKE
* 180ml (¾ cup) vegetable oil, plus a little extra for brushing
* 225g (2¼ cups) self-raising (self-rising) flour
* 275g (1¼ cups) caster (superfine) sugar
* 2 teaspoons baking powder
* 90g (scant 1 cup) cocoa powder
* 3 eggs
* 180ml (¾ cup) milk

FOR THE ICING (FROSTING)
* 250ml (generous 1 cup) double (heavy) cream
* 250g (9oz) milk chocolate

TO DECORATE
* Lots of sprinkles
* Lots of colourful sweets

< **SERVES** at least 12 >

1 Set the oven to 180°C/380°F/ Gas Mark 4.

3 Brush the sides and base of the tins with a little oil. Press the paper circles into the bases. Set aside.

4 To make the cake, just bung all the cake ingredients in a large mixing bowl and stir. It's that easy!

2 Place the cake tins on a sheet of baking paper, trace around them and cut out the circles.

Don't do what we did and almost forget the eggs! Or argue about who does what.

5 Use a whisk to get the batter really smooth.

6 Divide the batter evenly between the 2 tins and smooth the tops with a spatula.

7 Carefully put into the oven (*GLOVES!*) – try to get them on the same rack. Set the timer for 25 minutes.

ADULT HELP ALERT!

8 They are ready when you stick a skewer in the middle and it comes out clean with no crumbs on it. Leave in the tins for 5 minutes and then carefully turn out onto a wire rack. Leave to cool.

9 To make the icing, pour the cream into a small saucepan. Break up the chocolate and add to the pan.

10 Set the pan over a medium heat and stir until the chocolate has melted and it's thick and shiny. Don't let the mixture boil!

Cover the sides with sprinkles and decorate the top with sweets. It looks brilliant!

12 Splodge some icing in the middle of the cake and use a spatula to spread it all over. Place the other cake on top, press down gently and then add another big dollop of icing on top. Spread over the top and around the sides to cover completely.

11 Pour into a bowl and refrigerate for 30 minutes. The icing should be thick.

SHERBERT
DIPPERS

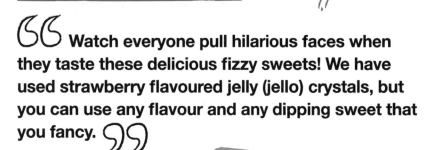

❝ **Watch everyone pull hilarious faces when they taste these delicious fizzy sweets! We have used strawberry flavoured jelly (jello) crystals, but you can use any flavour and any dipping sweet that you fancy.** ❞

TOP TIP
Tell the person who does the shopping you can buy citric acid from health food shops and pharmacies.

1 Sift the icing sugar and bicarbonate of soda into a bowl.

2 Add the citric acid and the strawberry jelly crystals and mix really well.

3 If these are for a party, carefully pour the sherbet into a food bag and add a dipper.

If using lollipops, tie the ribbon around the bag and the stick.

TOP TIP

To make a really yummy fizzy drink, put a tablespoon of the final sherbet into a glass of water.

4 Tie the bag up with ribbon.

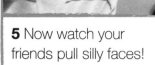

5 Now watch your friends pull silly faces!

INCREDIBLE

PARTY DRINKS

"These drinks are a special treat and not for drinking every day! They're really a drink and a dessert all in one, so you'll need a straw AND a spoon. "

Jiggle your straw to mix the cordial and soda. Gorgeous!

ICE CREAM SPIDER

* 2 scoops vanilla ice cream

* 2 tablespoons fruit juice cordial

* Soda water or lemonade

< MAKES 1 >

1 Scoop the ice cream into a tall glass and add the cordial.

2 Slowly pour in the soda water or lemonade so the bubbles rise above the top of the glass. Watch it foam and fizz!

SPOTTY CHOCOLATE BISCUIT MILKSHAKE

* 200ml (scant 1 cup) milk

* 1 or 2 tablespoons drinking chocolate

* 1 scoop vanilla or chocolate ice cream

* 1 chocolate biscuit (cookie)

* ½ teaspoon vanilla extract

* A few large marshmallows

< MAKES 1 >

ADULT HELP ALERT!

1 Carefully put the milk, drinking chocolate, ice cream, biscuit and vanilla extract in the bowl of a food processor or blender and blitz until there are no chunks of biscuit left.

2 Cut the marshmallows in half and firmly stick the gooey edge to the inside of a tall glass.

3 Pour the milkshake into the glass with the marshmallows. Delicious!

9

EDIBLE PRESENTS

CHOCOLATE ORANGE TRUFFLES
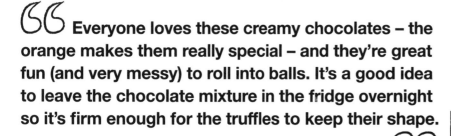

66 **Everyone loves these creamy chocolates – the orange makes them really special – and they're great fun (and very messy) to roll into balls. It's a good idea to leave the chocolate mixture in the fridge overnight so it's firm enough for the truffles to keep their shape.** 99

Oh dear... I must stop eating all the chocolate!

1 Break the chocolate into very small pieces and place in a heavy pan (and not in your mouth!). Keep the pan off the heat.

2 Add the butter, cream and golden syrup.

Just grate the orange bit, not the white pith.

3 Carefully grate the orange zest and add this to the pan of chocolate.

4 Set the pan over a medium-low heat and stir constantly with a wooden spoon until the chocolate has melted and it is smooth and luscious.

EPIC FAIL ALERT! Don't let it boil!

5 Carefully tip the mixture into a heatproof bowl. When it's cool, cover with cling film and chill in the fridge for at least 3 hours but preferably overnight. It needs to be able to hold its shape.

6 When the mixture's ready, spread the coatings you want to use onto separate plates.

7 You don't have to coat the truffles in anything if you don't want to, they'll still be yummy! If you're using cocoa, sift it first.

8 Use a teaspoon or a melon baller to scoop out little balls of the truffle mixture.

9 Briefly roll in the palms of your hands then lightly roll in a coating. Place in a sweet case.

10 Keep in the fridge. Give them away in a pretty box if you like.

NANNA ESTHER'S ROCKY ROAD

YOU NEED

* Oil, for brushing
* 90g (3oz) jelly sweets
* 20g (¾oz) popcorn (shop bought or see opposite for how to make from scratch)
* 75g (2½oz) mini marshmallows
* 250g (9oz) milk chocolate
* 100g (3½oz) dark chocolate
* 35g (1¼oz) butter

< **MAKES** 16 squares >

" **This rocky road is SO good and a little bit different because it has crunchy popcorn in it. Wrap in greaseproof paper, tie with a ribbon and you've got the perfect present for someone with a sweet tooth!** "

1 Line a 20 x 20cm (8 x 8in) baking tray with foil and brush with oil.

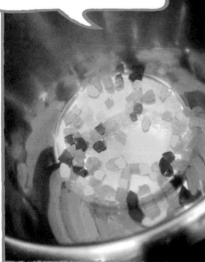

4 Break both types of chocolate up into small pieces and place in a heatproof bowl big enough to sit over a pan – a metal one is perfect.

2 If you're using larger jelly sweets cut them into small pieces. Place them in a large mixing bowl.

3 Add the popcorn and the marshmallows and gently stir so that everything is evenly mixed. Set aside.

This looks so good already!

Add the butter to the chocolate.

6 Half fill a small pan with water and bring to the boil over a high heat. When it starts to boil turn off the heat. Carefully place the bowl of chocolate on top of the pan, making sure it does not touch the water. Stir occasionally. You want it all to melt into a delicious goo.

8 Tip into the baking tray and spread out with the back of a wooden spoon, right into the corners of the tray. Leave to set in the fridge for 2–3 hours.

7 Carefully pour the chocolate over the dry ingredients and gently stir until everything is completely covered in chocolate.

9 Very carefully cut the rocky road into 16 squares and wrap or munch…

Do we have to give these away?!

These go quickly, so put aside any you want to give as gifts.

HOW TO POP CORN

* 3 tablespoons vegetable oil
* ½ cup popping corn

1 Heat the oil in a pan over a medium-high heat and add 4 of the kernels. Put the lid on.

2 When the kernels pop, pour in the rest of the kernels and cover with a lid. They'll soon start to pop like crazy.

3 ADULT HELP ALERT
Wearing oven gloves, keep shaking the pan until you can't hear much popping. Each pop will be about 3 seconds apart when ready.

4 Take the pan off the heat and shake a bit more – the stragglers might still pop.

EASY
LEMON CURD

66 **Our poppa loved this tangy lemon spread and every time we make it we think of him. In fact, all adults love this so it makes a really cool present – and an excellent way to impress your teacher if you give them a jar as a gift!** 99

BEFORE YOU BEGIN
You will need some clean, dry jars. This will fill 2 x 250ml (8½fl oz) jars or 1 x 500ml (17fl oz) jar. We used old pesto jars that we scrubbed really well!

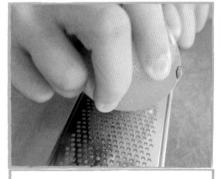

1 Very carefully grate the lemon zest of all 3 lemons. You just want the yellow part and not the white pith!

2 Cut each of the lemons in half and squeeze out all the juice using a lemon squeezer.

The lemons are a bit slippery without the skin so hold them tight.

3 Carefully cut the butter into small cubes.

4 Crack the eggs into a bowl and whisk them together using a fork.

5 Put the lemon juice, lemon zest, butter, eggs and sugar into a heatproof bowl that will sit on top of a small pan. Don't use a metal bowl for this as the mixture will get too hot.

6 Quarter-fill the pan with water and set it over a high heat until the water boils.

EPIC FAIL ALERT!
Only fill with a little water or the bowl will touch the water!

7 Reduce the heat to medium-low so that there are only gentle bubbles. Sit the bowl on top.

9 Gradually it will all melt together into a tasty yellow sauce. But keep stirring!

EPIC FAIL ALERT!
Be very careful that the water does not boil or simmer too fiercely or you will end up with lemon-flavoured scrambled eggs! If you think it is getting too hot turn the heat down!

8 Keep stirring the mixture with a wooden spoon.

10 This is where you need patience. Continue stirring for 5–10 minutes or until the sauce thickens.

will thicken lots ore as it cools.

1 Test to see if it's ready by ipping in a spatula or spoon. a nice coating sticks to the patula, and you can make a line own the middle with your finger, 's done.

12 Carefully pour the lemon curd into a jug and let cool. Fill your jar or jars not quite to the top. Put the lids on.

If the lemon curd's a present it's really nice to decorate with fabric and a colourful ribbon

This will last in the fridge for 1 week. It's wonderful spread on toast!

INDEX

ACKNOWLEDGEMENTS

This book is dedicated to my father, Terry, who discovered the joys of cooking late in life. Fun was an essential ingredient in everything he turned his hand to.

Huge thanks go to the lovely Anne Furniss for having faith in our idea and commissioning the book. Her support along the way was invaluable. I'm also indebted to Diana Henry and Catie Ziller for their constant encouragement.

Helen Lewis, Louise McKeever, Gemma Hayden, Katherine Case: thank you so much for arranging the pieces of this jigsaw so beautifully. I'm thrilled with the result and extremely grateful for your talents, patience and support.

Many thanks go to Luke Stuart, director and chef tutor at the wonderful White Pepper Cookery School in Dorset (www.white-pepper.co.uk). Thanks so much for sharing your expertise and helping us get our knife skills absolutely right.

Most importantly, this book would not have been possible without the help of so many kids!

Huge, huge, huge thanks go to: Zac and Charlie Newton-John, Sadie and Olive Quinn, Yollanda and Cameron Littleboy, Jack and Amara Moore, Charlie and Holly Naysmith, Finley and Jasper Hallett, Ethan and James King, Leo Rushbrook-Bates, Jack Seymour, Rudie Quinn, Olivia Downey, Millie Clark, Beth Perdrisat, Alice Christian-Edwards, Mia Santoni, Scarlett, Sapphire and Satine Thomson, Sasha Trijssenaar and George Byrnes Robertson.

Thanks as ever to my amazing husband and cameraman extraordinaire, Adam, for helping me get this idea off the ground and helping me through the mad and stressful process of making it happen. Not a photograph could have been taken without your guidance and patience. Not to mention lighting.

Finally, to my hardworking little chefs Ruby and Ben: words can't describe how proud I am of you both. The huge effort you put in to make this book was truly amazing – you worked without complaint and always a smile. A million times thank you my darlings – you're stars.

Editorial director Anne Furniss
Creative director Helen Lewis
Editors Louise McKeever and Sofie Shearman
Designers Gemma Hayden, Katherine Case
Photographer Sue Quinn
Production director Vincent Smith
Production controller Leonie Kellman

First published as *The Kids Only Cookbook* in 2013 by Quadrille Publishing Ltd

This edition published in 2024 by Quadrille Publishing Ltd

Quadrille
52–54 Southwark Street
London SE1 1UN
www.quadrille.com

Text © 2024 Sue Quinn
Photography © 2013 Sue Quinn
Design and layout © 2013 Quadrille Publishing Ltd

British Library Cataloguing-in-Publication Data
A catalogue record for this book is available from the British Library.

ISBN: 978 1 83783 277 4

Printed in China